D1098178

Published simultaneously in 1993 by Exley Publications in Great Britain, and Exley Giftbooks in the USA.

**Picture and text selection by © Helen Exley 1993.**
**Border Illustrations © Sharon Bassin 1993.**
ISBN 1-85015-451-1

Edited by Helen Exley.
Illustrated by Sharon Bassin.
Designed by Pinpoint Design.
Picture research by Image Select.
Printed in China

12  11  10  9  8  7  6  5  4  3

Exley Publications Ltd, 16 Chalk Hill, Watford, Herts WD1 4BN, United Kingdom.

Exley Giftbooks, 232 Madison Avenue, Suite 1206, New York, NY 10016, USA.

Acknowledgements: The publishers gratefully acknowledge permission to reproduce copyright material, and would be interested to hear from any copyright holders not here acknowledged.
PAM BROWN, "Surprises from Devizes", "Day or Night", "Annie and Edith", "What is a Friend?" definitions; ANGELA DOUGLAS, "Sounding Board". Extract from an article in *She* magazine, June 1985. Reprinted with permission of John Farquharson Ltd; KAHLIL GIBRAN, "On Friendship". Reprinted from *The Prophet*, by Kahlil Gibran, by permission of Alfred A. Knopf Inc. Copyright 1923 by Kahlil Gibran and renewed 1951 by Administrators C.T.A. of the Kahlil Gibran Estate and Mary G. Gibran; CHARLOTTE GRAY, "Someone long parted...", "Another Spring"; IRISH TOASTS, from *Sláinte, your book of Irish Toasts and Irish Whiskey,* © Copyright 1980, Irish Distillers Group PLC, reprinted with permission; HELEN KELLER, "Red-Letter Days" from *My Religion*. Reprinted courtesy of the Swedenborg Foundation, New York NY 10010, copyright 1960, USA; JOHN MACDONALD, "When you don't edit yourself" from *Bright Orange for the Shroud*. Reprinted with permission of John Farquharson Ltd. and Alfred A. Knopf Inc; WAYNE MACKEY, quote from *The Oklahoma City Times,* copyright The Oklahoma Publishing Company; HENRY ALONZO MYERS, "Bound To Us In Triumph and Disaster". Reprinted from Henry Alonzo Myers: *Are Men Equal? An Inquiry into the Meaning of American Democracy.* © Copyright, 1945 by Henry Alonzo Myers. Used by permission of the publisher, Cornell University Press.

Picture Credits: AKG: cover and pages 10, 17, 25, 36/37. Art Museum of Atenaum, Helsinki: page 47. Bridgeman Art Library: title page and pages 8, 12, 30, 41, 47. Chris Beetles: page 22/23. Christopher Wood Gallery: pages 31 and 51. Fine Art Photographic Library Ltd: pages 15, 20, 22, 26, 28, 34, 39, 42, 45, 49, 53, 57, 58/59, 61. Fine Art Society London: page 51. Guildhall Art Gallery: page 13. Museums at Stony Brook: page 41. Scala: page 34. Wolverhampton Art Gallery: page 8.

# *Thank heavens for* FRIENDS

**EXLEY**

NEW YORK · WATFORD, UK

# FRIENDS!

It is a good thing to be rich, and a good thing to be strong, but it is a better thing to be beloved of many friends.

*EURIPIDES*

Friendship is unnecessary, like philosophy, like art . . . It has no survival value; rather it is one of those things that give value to survival.

*C.S. LEWIS*

Who seeks a friend without a fault remains without one.

*PROVERB FROM THE TURKISH*

Go often to the house of thy friend; for weeds soon choke up the unused path.

*EDDA [SCANDINAVIAN MYTHOLOGY]*

One does not make friends; one recognizes them.

*ISABEL PATERSON*

I don't need a friend who changes when I change and who nods when I nod; my shadow does that much better.

*PLUTARCH*

God gave us our relatives: thank God we can choose our friends.

*ETHEL WATTS MUMFORD*

# DEFINITIONS OF FRIENDSHIP

The most I can do for my friend is simply to be
his friend. I have no wealth to bestow on him.
If he knows that I am happy in loving him, he
will want no other reward. Is not friendship
divine in this?

*HENRY DAVID THOREAU*

A friend is the one who comes in when the whole
world has gone out.

*ALBAN GOODIER*

Treat your friends as you do your pictures, and
place them in their best light.

*JENNIE JEROME CHURCHILL*

Nothing more dangerous than a friend without
discretion; even a prudent enemy is preferable.

*JEAN DE LA FONTAINE*

The making of friends, who are real friends,
is the best token we have of a person's success
in life.

*EDWARD EVERETT HALE*

Do not save your loving speeches
For your friends till they are dead;
Do not write them on their tombstones,
Speak them rather now instead.

*ANNA CUMMINS*

# A FRIEND IS . . .

A friend is one who incessantly pays us the compliment of expecting from us all the virtues, and who can appreciate them in us.

The friend asks no return but that his friend will religiously accept and wear and not disgrace his apotheosis of him. They cherish each other's hopes. They are kind to each other's dreams.

That kindness which has so good a reputation elsewhere can least of all consist with this relation, and no such affront can be offered to a friend, as a conscious good-will, a friendliness which is not a necessity of the friend's nature.

Friendship is never established as an understood relation. It is a miracle which requires constant proofs. It is an exercise of the purest imagination and of the rarest faith.

We do not wish for friends to feed and clothe our bodies – neighbors are kind enough for that – but to do the life office to our spirit. For this, few are rich enough, however well disposed they may be . . . .

The language of friendship is not words, but meanings. It is an intelligence above language.

**HENRY DAVID THOREAU**

# A FRIEND

A friend is a present you give yourself.

ROBERT LOUIS STEVENSON

I no doubt deserved my enemies, but I don't believe I deserved my friends.

WALT WHITMAN

If two people who love each other let a single instant wedge itself between them, it grows – it becomes a month, a year, a century; it becomes too late.

JEAN GIRAUDOUX

I do not wish to treat friendships daintily, but with roughest courage. When they are real, they are not glass threads or frost-work, but the solidest thing we know.

RALPH WALDO EMERSON

. . . when people have light in themselves, it will shine out from them. Then we get to know each other as we walk together in the darkness, without needing to pass our hands over each other's faces, or to intrude into each other's hearts.

ALBERT SCHWEITZER

## *from* "THE PROPHET"

And a youth said, Speak to us of Friendship.
And he answered, saying:
Your friend is your needs answered.
He is your field which you sow with love and
    reap with thanksgiving.
And he is your board and your fireside.
For you come to him with your hunger, and
    you seek him for peace.

When your friend speaks his mind you fear not
    the "nay" in your own mind, nor do you
    withhold the "ay".
And when he is silent your heart ceases not to
    listen to his heart;
For without words, in friendship, all thoughts,
    all desires, all expectations are born and
    shared, with joy that is unacclaimed.
When you part from your friend, you grieve not;
For that which you love most in him may be
    clearer in his absence, as the mountain to the
    climber is clearer from the plain.
And let there be no purpose in friendship save
    the deepening of the spirit.
For love that seeks aught but the disclosure of
    its own mystery is not love but a net cast forth:
    and only the unprofitable is caught.

And let your best be for your friend.

If he must know the ebb of your tide, let him
    know its flood also.

For what is your friend that you should seek him
    with hours to kill?

Seek him always with hours to live.

For it is his to fill your need, but not your
    emptiness.

And in the sweetness of friendship let there be
    laughter, and sharing of pleasures.

For in the dew of little things the heart finds
    its morning and is refreshed.

*KAHLIL GIBRAN, "THE PROPHET"*

# THE GIFT OF FRIENDSHIP

I know now that the world is not filled with strangers. It is full of other people – waiting only to be spoken to.

BETH DAY

. . . to find a friend one must close one eye: to keep him, two.

NORMAN DOUGLAS

First of all things, for friendship, there must be that delightful, indefinable state called feeling at ease with your companion, – the one man, the one woman out of a multitude who interests you, who meets your thoughts and tastes.

JULIA DUHRING

Anybody can sympathize with the sufferings of a friend, but it requires a very fine nature to sympathize with a friend's success.

OSCAR WILDE

But of all plagues, good Heaven, thy wrath can send,
Save me, oh, save me, from the candid friend.

GEORGE CANNING

Instead of loving your enemies, treat your friends a little better.

EDGAR WATSON HOWE

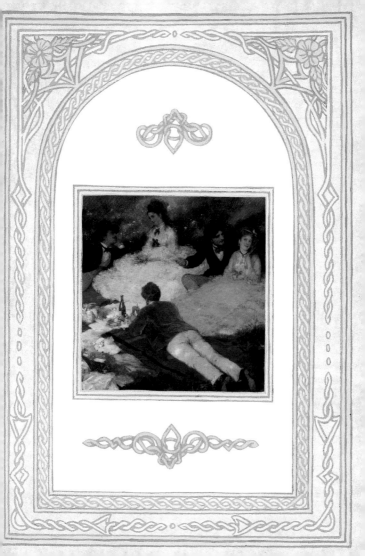

## MISCELLANEOUS FILE

Just why should friends be chronological,
Fraternal friends, or pedagogical,
Alike in race or taste or color –
It only makes the meetings duller!
Unclassified by tribe or steeple,
Why shouldn't friends be merely people?

*DOROTHY BROWN THOMPSON*

Little friends may prove great friends.

*AESOP*

# WITHOUT A WORD, WITHOUT A SIGN

I love you not only for what you are,
but for what I am when I am with you.

I love you not only for what you have made
of yourself, but for what you are making of me.

I love you because you have done more than
    any creed
could have done to make me good, and more
than any fate could have done to make me happy.

You have done it without a touch,
without a word, without a sign.

You have done it by being yourself. Perhaps
that is what being a friend means, after all.

**ANONYMOUS**

# WHEN SILENCE IS BEYOND WORDS

There may be moments in friendship, as in love, when silence is beyond words. The faults of our friend may be clear to us, but it is well to seem to shut our eyes to them. Friendship is usually treated by the majority of people as a tough and everlasting thing which will survive all manner

of bad treatment. But this is an exceedingly
great and foolish error; it may die in an hour of a
single unwise word; its conditions of existence
are that it should be dealt with delicately and
tenderly, being as it is a sensible plant and not a
roadside thistle. We must not expect our friend
to be above humanity.

*OUIDA*

# SOUNDING-BOARD

What is a friend to me? In the simplest terms, it's someone who will allow me to be the way I am and not think me totally round the bend. Someone who can tell by the look on my face when I need to talk about what's happening, or not happening, in my life. Someone who provides non-judgmental support. It is extremely therapeutic to have the opportunity to discuss problems, to consider possibilities, to use friends as a sounding-board, in order to see your problems differently. A friend is someone who needs me, trusts me, and is happy when my news is good; someone who won't go away.

I was brought up to be Miss Priss, Miss Shockable. But I was also brought up to challenge my values. My parents taught me that the world may take your money, your home, your livelihood . . . so what? Friends should be treasured. And to have good friends, you must *be* a good friend. That's what mother told me. As always, she was right.

ANGELA DOUGLAS

## ... AGAINST ALL THE EVILS OF LIFE

Life is to be fortified by many friendships.
To love, and to be loved, is the greatest happiness.
If I lived under the burning sun of the equator, it
would be pleasure for me to think that there were
many human beings on the other side of the world
who regarded and respected me; I could not live if
I were alone upon the earth, and cut off from the
remembrance of my fellow-creatures. It is not that
a person has occasion often to fall back upon the
kindness of friends; perhaps we may never
experience the necessity of doing so; but we are
governed by our imaginations, and they stand
there as a solid and impregnable bulwark against
all the evils of life.

*Sydney Smith*

# RED-LETTER DAYS

There are red-letter days in our lives when we meet people who thrill us like a fine poem, people whose handshake is brimful of unspoken sympathy and whose sweet, rich natures impart to our eager, impatient spirits a wonderful restfulness . . . . Perhaps we never saw them before and they may never cross our life's path again; but the influence of their calm, mellow natures is a libation poured upon our discontent, and we feel its healing touch as the ocean feels the mountain stream freshening its brine . . . .

*HELEN KELLER*

His thoughts were slow,
His words were few,
   and never formed to glisten.
But he was a joy to all his friends –
You should have heard him listen.

QUOTED BY WAYNE MACKEY
IN OKLAHOMA CITY TIMES

# ANOTHER SPRING

Friendships fail some years,
blight twists the leaves and the crop is bitter.
Frost bites
or sudden fire devours:
but the root lies sound
and waits for better weather
or a storm of sleet to scour the branches.
Then we shall see another spring:
a flare of green flame
and flowers burning to fruit
along the boughs.

*CHARLOTTE GRAY*

# WHEN YOU DON'T EDIT YOURSELF

A friend is someone to whom you can say any jackass thing that enters your mind. With acquaintances, you are forever aware of their slightly unreal image of you, and you edit yourself to fit. Many marriages are between acquaintances. You can be with a person for three hours of your life and have a friend. Another one will remain an acquaintance for thirty years.

**J.D. MacDonald**

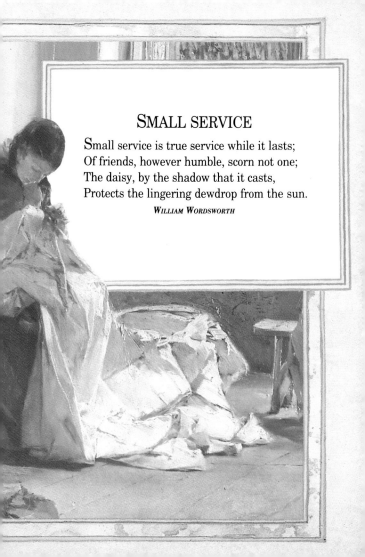

# SMALL SERVICE

Small service is true service while it lasts;
Of friends, however humble, scorn not one;
The daisy, by the shadow that it casts,
Protects the lingering dewdrop from the sun.

*WILLIAM WORDSWORTH*

Oh, the comfort, the inexpressible comfort, of feeling safe with a person; having neither to weigh thoughts nor measure words, but to pour them all out just as they are, chaff and grain together, knowing that a faithful hand will take and sift them, keep what is worth keeping, and then, with the breath of kindness, blow the rest away.

*GEORGE ELIOT (MARY ANN EVANS)*

The friends thou hast, and their adoption tried,
Grapple them to thy soul with hoops of steel;
But do not dull thy palm with entertainment
Of each new-hatch'd, unfledg'd comrade. Beware
Of entrance to a quarrel; but being in,
Bear't that th'opposed may beware of thee.
Give every man thine ear, but few thy voice;
Take each man's censure, but reserve thy
    judgment . . .
Neither a borrower, nor a lender be;
For loan oft loses itself and friend,
And borrowing dulls the edge of husbandry.
This above all: to thine own self be true,
And it must follow, as the night the day,
Thou canst not then be false to any man.

**WILLIAM SHAKESPEARE**

## from "A CHILD'S VIEW OF HAPPINESS"

Happiness is if you give it away.

**CHRISTOPHER HOARE, 11**

Happiness is giving a little and taking a little, even if it is a mere dandelion. It is worth a bouquet of red roses wrapped in delicate lace if it is given with care.

**HELEN CADDICK, 11**

I like to see the persons face light up with joy, and the rustling of the wrapping paper being torn off of the present. It's so nice when they thank you for the present, and that warms you all over.

**PAUL OWEN, 13**

Happiness is my friend's hand.

*GILLIAN QUEEN, 10*

Happiness is the whole world as friends. It's light all through your life.

*DANIEL DILLING, 8*

Happiness is like a disease. It spreads.

*SIMON ELLIOT, 11*

It costs nothing to say a "hello" here and there.
To friends that you pass in the street.
It costs nothing to smile at a stranger,
Or at any new friend that you meet.
It costs nothing to show your emotions,
or your feelings when things don't go right.
It costs nothing to help the unfortunate,
Who are blind or who have no sight.
It costs nothing to be happy.
And happiness can be found.
Happiness is like butter,
So go on and spread some around.

*JEANETTE ACHILLES, 15*

Some people have a beautiful smile and when people see it they feel happy.

*SUSANNAH MORRIS, 10*

# WITHOUT FRIENDS

Without friends no one would choose to live, though he had all other goods; even rich people, and those in possession of office and of dominating power are thought to need friends most of all; for what is the use of such prosperity without the opportunity of beneficence, which is exercised chiefly and in its most laudable form towards friends? Or how can prosperity be guarded and preserved without friends? The greater it is, the more exposed it is to risk. And in poverty and in other misfortunes people think friends are the only refuge. It helps the young, too, to keep from error; it aids older people by ministering to their needs and supplementing the activities that are failing from weakness; those in the prime of life it stimulates to noble actions . . . for with friends people are more able both to think and to act.

*ARISTOTLE*

# WHAT IS A FRIEND?

Friends don't even notice the body you are living in.

Friends are people who go on conspiratorial shopping sprees together, diving in and out of shops totally beyond their price range, and ending up eating oozing cream cakes with only just enough money to get home.

Friends don't actually lie for each other – but they put down very good smoke screens.

A friend never mentions a *thing* to old blabbermouth over the road.

Everyone half hopes there's a heaven – just to put things right with old friends.

Acquaintances call nervously to ask if they can do anything to help. Friends come and sit with your horribly infectious kids while you dash off to the Denver concert.

Friends don't have to be good looking or sexy – come to think of it, maybe that's why they are friends.

Love is blind; friendship quietly closes its eyes.

A friend is the one person who can correct your faults – and has the sense not to try.

It's easier to love mankind than keep a few friendships in good repair.

Love links two lives inextricably, like Siamese twins. Friendship lets you walk comfortably side by side.

**PAM BROWN**

## BOUND TO US IN TRIUMPH AND DISASTER

On the level of the human spirit an equal, a companion, an understanding heart is one who can share a person's point of view. What this means we all know. Friends, companions, lovers, are those who treat us in terms of our unlimited worth to ourselves. They are closest to us who best understand what life means to us, who feel for us as we feel for ourselves, who are bound to us in triumph and disaster, who break the spell of our loneliness.

*HENRY ALONZO MYERS*

# "HE'S ALIVE!"

Two miners in a mine in New Mexico had placed eleven charges of dynamite at the bottom of an eighty-five-foot shaft, and prepared their fuses with enough time to scramble up to the higher levels, where they would be protected from the blast. Then things went terrifyingly wrong. With the fuses burning, the first miner, Carl Myers, reached safety. But before his mate Harry Reid reached the protected area, one of the charges went off. Harry was punched down by the blast, knocked unconscious, wounded by hundreds of splinters driven into his legs. Carl called frantically. No reply. And the rest of those sticks of dynamite were seconds away from exploding, with certain death for Harry. Carl hurled himself back down the slope again, gathered his unconscious friend onto his back and started to claw his way back up the slope to safety, every sinew in his body pounding under the strain, every second ticking in his brain. As he reached the top – and collapsed to safety – the dynamite ripped the mountain. The company Carl and Harry worked for wanted to sponsor Carl for the Carnegie Award for Heroism. Carl was having none of it. "Damn the medal," he muttered. "He's alive, isn't he?"

*Richard Alan*

# THIS <u>PARTICULAR</u> PERSON MATTERS

It is a mistake to think that one makes a friend because of his or her qualities, it has nothing to do with qualities at all. It is the person that we want, not what he does or says, or does not do or say, but what he or she *is* that is eternally enough! Who shall explain the extraordinary instinct that tells us, perhaps after a single meeting, that this or that particular person in some mysterious way matters to us? I confess that, for myself, I never enter a new company without the hope that I may discover a friend, perhaps *the* friend, sitting there with an expectant smile. That hope survives a thousand disappointments. People who deal with life generously and large-heartedly go on multiplying relationships to the end.

**ARTHUR CHRISTOPHER BENSON**

## OLD FRIENDS

Old friends are the great blessing of one's latter
years. Half a word conveys one's meaning. They
have a memory of the same events, and have the
same mode of thinking. I have young relations
that may grow upon me, for my nature is
affectionate, but can they grow old friends?

*HORACE WALPOLE*

# ANNIE AND EDITH

Annie and Edith had known each other from the time when their skinny adolescent bodies were packed and laced and buttoned into their black, bustled frocks and their bony little feet crammed into button-hooked boots. Annie became cook to a lord, and Edith the wife of a Guardsman, to which positions they brought the gusto and doggedness and shrewd, pawky humour of their kind. Annie was the more volatile, having French blood, and frequently left home, with no ill effects to her family, as they knew quite well where she was. She was with Edith, getting it all out of her system and drinking quantities of strong tea.

Widowed, they got the weeping over with and tore even more ferociously into living. Edith took to Speedway, Annie to the Horses. Annie still left home at regular intervals, and the two of them went on minor rampages to the seaside, the black-eyed Annie and the china-blue-eyed Edith out for the day. Cockles, whelks, shrimp teas, milk stout and a little jay walking. Any guardian angels they may have had sweated as they wove their way among the crowds, crossing roads against the lights and giving young policemen lip. They never became the least drunk or disorderly. They simply had a very good time, frequently ending up adopted by teenagers out on the spree, being fed rock salmon and chips, and allowed to sit on the motorbikes.

They were grandmas to be relished, for they had about them a rollicking piratical air that other grans had not.

Edith died first, indignant at eighty-two to find herself suddenly old. It was a raggle-taggle funeral with all manner of unexpected people turning up, and unexpected things going wrong. Engineered, one suspected, by Edith.

Annie looked paler and more French than ever. Dressed in tight black, she wept for her ancient ally, unnerved by this abrupt silence, this assumption of dignity.

She did not last long afterwards. Ordinary people were too dull to detain her.

God knows what the pair of them are up to now.

*PAM BROWN*

# DAY OR NIGHT

What have I got for you, my friend?

The last flowers from a winter garden, to shine against the dark. The recipe you asked for. An envelope of seeds. An empty perfume bottle for your little girl. A slice of cold bread pudding. A glossy magazine, found on a train. Scones hot from the oven. Jam hot from the stove. A small striped kitten if you want him. An armchair past its prime, to lend a little comfort to your son's first home. A glass of wine. A dab of scent. Half a box of bedding plants.

A pair of hands, a mop and comfort when the washing machine runs berserk.

A back to brace the wardrobe you intend to shift.

A shoulder very like you mom's to cry on.

The episode of a soap you missed, in total recall.

Coffee.

First aid.

An extension of your own vocabulary in times of indignation.

News of the local otter.

Availability. Day or night.

**PAM BROWN**

## OLD COATS, OLD FRIENDS

My coat and I live comfortably together. It has
assumed all my wrinkles, does not hurt me
anywhere, has moulded itself on my deformities,
and is complacent to all my movements, and I
only feel its presence because it keeps me warm.
Old coats and old friends are the same thing.

*VICTOR HUGO*

# IRISH TOASTS

May the frost never afflict your spuds.
May the outside leaves of your cabbage
always be free from worms.
May the crows never pick your haystack,
and may your donkey always be in foal.

Health and long life to you.
The husband of your choice to you.
A child every year to you.
Land without rent to you.
And may you be half-an-hour in heaven
before the devil knows you're dead.
* Sláinte!

May you live as long as you want
and never want as long as you live!

May you die in bed at 95 years,
shot by a jealous wife.

May you have warm words on a cold evening,
a full moon on a dark night,
and a smooth road all the way to your door.

May the road rise to meet you.
May the wind be always at your back,
the sun shine warm upon your face,
the rain fall soft upon your fields,
and until we meet again
may God hold you in the hollow of His hand.

*from "Slainte!"*

\* *Health*

# Contempt

It has long been known that Woody Allen, understandably, does not enjoy being the constant center of attention of his fans. The idea that he might feel disdain for his public, however, was not widely considered until the release in 1980 of *Stardust Memories*. *Stardust* seems to be a particularly self-revelatory movie, and several of the men and women interviewed for *I Dream of Woody* had pre-*Stardust* dreams that anticipated the mood of the film. Fred Forman's wonderful, sad dream in which Dream Woody calls everyone Fred portrays Woody's need to separate himself from his audience. "They all look alike," Dream Woody implied of his fans. And Lyn Rubin's less-controlled Dream Woody threw up on her because, much to her shame, she didn't have anything worthwhile to say. The dreams below show how different fans respond to Dream Woody's contempt.

•

**PAULINE BANKS** is a twenty-six-year-old psychologist who grew up in the Chicago suburbs. She characterizes New York as "a seductive city with a lot to offer," but, she says, "you have to pay for it." She was able to describe Woody Allen in the same terms in her dream from the fall of 1978.

### THE MAKE-OVER

My husband and I were having dinner in a restaurant on the ground floor of a brownstone. The room was large with heavy wooden

**143**

beams. We both liked this place because it didn't scream at us. It was posh, but subtle.

Woody Allen approached our table, introduced himself and then told me: "I'm going to make you a star.

"Not a star in the glamorous Hollywood sense," he continued. "Rather, I'd like to help you to buy some clothes, make some contacts, and fill out what you're already doing for yourself." He then told me whom to contact, and left.

I did it. In the following weeks I bought new clothes; I had a makeup consultation; I became polished; and I went to parties with stimulating, hard-to-reach people. Woody had financially underwritten all of this and provided the intros. There had been no contact from Woody himself, however. But one day, a couple of months after our original meeting, I ran into him.

"You look total, now," Woody said coldly. He nodded, indicating that he was pleased with his work. I could feel his satisfaction in his own power. He gave me a cruel glance and walked away.

Woody's total awareness of his own manipulations chilled me. I woke up cold and cynical.

Pauline's dream benefactor sounds more like J. R. Ewing than the Woody persona we're accustomed to seeing in the movies. Pauline was puzzled by her dream. But she thinks that "it may show the way he really is." More than a few Allen fans share Pauline's suspicions that the filmmaker in real life is more calculating and less helpless than he would have his audience believe, and they find themselves struggling to reconcile two aspects of his personality: the sensitive, anxious man with moral and artistic integrity and the shrewd, controlling man. Of course, shrewdness and vulnerability can go hand in hand in one personality; in fact, it's an effective combination, as Woody Allen has demonstrated. Still, discovering this about an idol can be unsettling.

•

**STU SANDERS** is an author who lectures widely and thinks of himself as "a professional Jew." Stu considers Woody Allen to be "a role model for nonmacho men" like himself. Explaining the breakup of his first marriage, Stu says: "She subscribed to *Playboy* and I subscribed to *Ms.*" Stu's identification with Allen has been constructive for him in other ways as well. He had been disturbed for a while by the fact that, although he was not yet thirty years old, he'd been divorced twice. Being divorced once was acceptable to him, but two divorces seemed to mean that something was wrong with him. Stu relaxed about his marital status once he remembered that Woody Allen also had been divorced twice.

Stu would prefer not to meet Allen because he respects the artist's right to privacy. He had the following dream on two occasions in 1978.

## STARDUST SYNAGOGUE

I learned that Woody Allen and I were scheduled to give lectures at the same time in the same synagogue.

"I'd rather go listen to *him* talk," I thought on my way to the synagogue.

I arrived at the synagogue and looked into the room where I was to lecture. A good number of people were in attendance. I thought there must be some mistake.

I went back out and checked the posted rooms to be sure that I had the correct one. I had. There was even a large poster reading "Woody Speaks Tonight" and pointing to the other room. These people had chosen to come to my lecture instead of Woody Allen's!

I returned to my audience—a typical, mostly middle-aged synagogue audience—and began my talk. As I looked out onto my audience, I felt, at first, a sense of pride. But my satisfaction soon dissipated.

I became aware that I really didn't like these people in my audience. In fact, I felt contempt for them.

"What kind of fools," I thought, "would come to see me instead of Woody Allen?"

Stu's remark at the end of his dream is similar to the Groucho Marx joke that Woody Allen as Alvy Singer tells in *Annie Hall*: "I would never wanna belong to any club that would have someone like me for a member."

Stu says that in real life he sometimes resents his audiences and that he is afraid of his own power with them. "How easily they're manipulated!" Stu's is a constructive dream, calling to his attention his feelings about his audiences. However, in this feeling, Stu seems to be identifying with Woody Allen in a destructive way, justifying his own contempt for his audience by what he perceives to be his role model's attitudes.

•

**BEANIE ALSTON** is a character actress who went to Woody Allen's open call for *Stardust Memories*. Beanie admires but does not envy Allen and is "heartened that he's no longer making such a big deal about his psychotherapy." In her dream, from April 12, 1978, Beanie identifies with Dream Woody's supercilious air.

### MR. ALLEN'S ANGRY BROW

I was making my way across Manhattan when I saw a large crowd gathered outside the Murray Hill Cinema. Between the crowd and me were three figures: Woody Allen, Diane Keaton and Ted Hook, the show-biz restaurateur.

Ted was interviewing Mr. Allen. And Diane Keaton was trying to shield Mr. Allen from both the crowd and from Ted Hook.

I couldn't help but notice that Ted and Woody Allen were both talking out of the sides of their mouths—literally. Ted Hook's words were angled toward the police barricade and the crowd, while Mr. Allen's words were angled toward me. Mr. Allen could tell that those monkeys behind the police barricade wouldn't understand what he was saying even if they heard him.

Ted, playing ringmaster, was trying to give the impression to the crowd that not only was he interviewing Woody Allen but he also had a very personal relationship with him. Mr. Allen, on the other hand, was just going through the motions of the interview, with a sense of obligation.

This charade went on for a few minutes. Then Ted Hook rushed busily toward the waiting throng. Meanwhile, Diane Keaton wiped Mr. Allen's angry brow.

I took this opportunity to approach Mr. Allen boldly, even though I shared Ms. Keaton's belief that this crowd of vultures was doing an injustice to the man. I held out my hand.

"Mr. Allen," I began, with a gesture of respect and a look of admiration.

A look of admiration then crossed Mr. Allen's face as he looked up at me.

"Beanie?" he said.

•

**ED BROWNSTEIN** is a classical pianist who recently made his New York debut and who, above all else, desires to be renowned. "My [career] is less related to my love of the art of music than it is to my wanting to be extremely successful and renowned. If I could do it through being a football player, I would pursue that just as actively. Or through being a chess champion—you know, it doesn't really matter that much— music just seems like the most accessible route to becoming famous." Ed would also like to be Woody Allen's friend. He had the following dream on New Year's Eve, 1979.

_____ **HAVE WE MET?** _____

I was walking through some large space in a building; it was something like a loft. The room was fairly well lit. There were lots of people and we were walking in one direction. But there were no people in my immediate vicinity. I was by myself.

The occasion was a piano competition. And we were all headed toward one end of the room because that's where the staircase was. The stairs led down into the basement, where the final event of the competition was going to be held. I, regrettably, had not entered the competition.

As I walked in the direction of the staircase, I noticed a piano. There was a railing behind the piano that set it off from the rest of the room. There was nobody in this immediate area, and so I went on over to the piano and started playing.

I was playing a Bach concerto when out of the corner of my eye I noticed this guy who seemed to be rather well dressed, rather conservatively dressed.

After eight or ten measures I looked up, and then I stopped playing. The guy was Woody Allen. He looked at me approvingly, and then he said some approving words about my music. I was quite flattered by his compliments.

We talked for a while at the piano. I pointed out to Woody that his works have great psychiatric significance. He was still listening to me, as we started walking toward the staircase together, on our way to the event.

I really was talking quite a bit. At one point I said to Woody, "That scene with the foot thing in _Love and Death_—I found that scene was highly analytific, not to mention platific." The truth is there isn't any foot thing in _Love and Death_. Woody halted and looked at me. He was trying to be polite, but he furrowed his face a bit, as though to say, "Jesus Christ, spare me!"

By now we were walking down the stairs. I was walking faster and Woody was lingering back. Then, at the bottom of the stairs, a violinist whom I know appeared and told me that you didn't have to have been in the competition to play in this final event. "Oh, gee," I said, "this means that I can play the Bach!" I started to rush to the room, eager to play in the event. Then I saw that Woody Allen was still behind me. Remembering his previous compliments, I turned to him and said enthusiastically: "I hope that if you stay around, you can hear me play!"

Woody's eyes widened. "Oh? You play?" he asked me.

Dream Woody gives and then takes away in this dream, as he has done in others. Ed thinks the Woody Allen in his dream was like his father. Ed has always wanted to please his father with his piano playing. But "my father is impossible to impress." Dream Woody, of course, was initially impressed with Ed's piano playing. It was only Ed's bogus erudition ("I found that scene was highly analytific, not to mention platific") that turned off Dream Woody (as phoniness repels film persona Woody and real-life Woody). Ed recognizes through Dream Woody's reaction how pretentious he's been and the dream takes a turn for the better. Once Ed acknowledges his foolishness, he gets to play in the competition. But then Dream Woody insults Ed, seems, within a matter of minutes, to have forgotten totally that Ed plays the piano! Perhaps this apparent injustice, plus the fact that the competition is held in the basement, is a comment (from Ed's unconscious) on the significance Ed attaches to his piano playing in his waking life.

●

**GUY JOHNSON** is a twenty-eight-year-old freshman at UCLA who has seen *Annie Hall* "only seven times." He recently wrote a term paper in which he interpreted Shakespeare's work in the context of Woody Allen's philosophy. "It was a boring subject and I wanted to liven it up," he says. In his dream, from spring 1980, Guy and Woody Allen share a private joke.

### _____ THE GREAT MARSHALL BRICKMAN HOAX _____

I was in Europe with some American friends. We had rented a really tiny European car and were driving through either France or Germany. It was pouring rain, and although it was very pretty, it was too much of a downpour to continue driving.

We parked the car by a little baroque-style candy shop and ran inside. There was an old-fashioned wooden counter and a lot of different candies under glass. Most of the candies were chocolate. I was looking the candy over—I'm a real chocolate freak—and there I saw Woody Allen, all by himself, also desirously eyeing the chocolates.

I thought: "Wow! This is my big chance to ask Woody Allen a question I've always wanted to know the answer to." I don't know how many films Woody has co-written with Marshall Brickman, but I've always wondered whether the guy really existed or whether he's just a joke.

I went up to speak to Woody and I tried to be cool about it. I didn't want to seem like a teenybopper, so I just said: "You know, I've seen all of your films and I've always wondered, who is Marshall Brickman?"

Woody answered me right away, without any hesitation. "Marshall Brickman doesn't exist," he said.

I felt good that my suspicion had turned out to be true, and I think Woody was impressed that I'd picked up on the joke.

Guy has since found out that Marshall Brickman, whom Dream Woody reduced to the fullest extent possible, is, indeed, a real person.

•

**BILL DARLINGTON** is a graduate student, an aspiring writer, who had once wanted to be "someone like Woody Allen—someone genuine and very natural." When he thought of Woody he thought of the "moral Woody." But, like many fans, Bill felt betrayed by *Stardust Memories*. He had the following dream on October 22, 1980, one week after seeing the movie.

—————————— **ANOTHER CHANCE** ——————————

Woody and I were watching his new movie *Stardust Memories*. Only this movie was not at all like the real-life film.

The *Stardust Memories* Woody and I were screening was in black and white, but it was also in 3-D! The story involved an alien giant who had come to earth to wipe out all life.

Woody, in a robot's metal suit, battled the giant until the monster fell to the ground as though defeated. It was a very funny scene.

The movie had a lot of action, including a fast chase scene in which Woody raced through a ditch between two highways, past some cars, over some grass, and in and out of a tunnel.

The movie had its good moments, but it was not well received. Not at all. Woody was depressed after the screening. He was listless and genuinely saddened.

The two of us sat down outside the screening room in a small tunnel-shaped room. The room seemed protective.

I wanted to reassure Woody. I took his hand and put both of my hands around it.

"Don't feel bad; I thought it was good," I told him.

Bill had not been willing, on a conscious level, to forgive Woody Allen for *Stardust Memories*. But his dream told him that, unconsciously, he wanted to forgive the filmmaker. Bill felt that in the dream he and Dream Woody were mutually protective of each other. The symbolism of the dream supports these themes: tunnels in dreams usually represent protection and/or the idea of being alone with one's unconscious. The dream movie is also consistent with the protection theme. Unlike the real *Stardust*, in which Allen portrays a character that some critics have labeled misanthropic, in Bill's *Stardust*, Dream Woody plays a character who protects mankind.

●

**MEG DAVIS** is a thirty-four-year-old New York lawyer. Meg celebrated passing her bar exam in 1976 with a week of dining and clubbing with friends. On Monday night she went to Michael's Pub to enjoy Woody Allen's New Orleans Funeral and Ragtime Jazz Band. She took with her a snapshot of Allen that she'd taken on a chance encounter near Central Park several months earlier.

It was break time for the band. Meg and a friend were having a drink at the crowded bar. Meg scribbled her name on the back of the out-of-focus snapshot and handed it along with a five-dollar bill to a passing waiter. "Will you please give this to Mr. Allen?" No problem.

Then the unexpected occurred. "Meg? Is anyone here named Meg?" A soft but distinctive voice could be heard through the crowd.

"Here," Meg said to Woody Allen.

"What is this picture? Do you want it back? Where—where is this?" he asked with apparent interest.

In spite of her years of verbal training in law school, Meg apparently wasn't quick enough with a stimulating response. "I said something like 'The picture is for you,'" Meg recalls. But more than anything else in this brief exchange, Meg remembers the astonishing speed with which Woody

Allen changed from being polite and curious to being coldly condescending. "He didn't say anything offensive," Meg said. "But by his facial expressions and his manner I felt scorned.... All this happened so quickly. And after he had chosen to come speak to me!"

How did Meg feel about the unpleasant experience with a filmmaker she had greatly respected? She says she considered a lot of excuses for Allen's behavior, and then she put the incident out of her mind. Until two years later. "I had a dream one night, and with the dream it all came back. For the first time I let myself feel the real disappointment I had experienced that night." Her dream is from 1978.

## LOSS OF INNOCENCE

I was doing volunteer clerical work in the crowded office of a legal aid group. Apparently I had been working on this project for a long time because I knew everyone on the staff rather well.

It was coffee break, and as I got up from the desk where I had been working, I mentioned that I was going to give Woody Allen a call. Everyone in the room instantly became excited and almost in a single voice demanded to know how I had obtained Woody's phone number! At this unexpected and somewhat accusing question, I became disoriented. I wasn't sure then that I actually did have his phone number. I defensively told my coworkers that I had seen Allen's number in *Show Biz*, a trade paper for actors. But I wasn't at all sure. By this time, I thought maybe I had imagined the whole thing, especially since I don't read *Show Biz*.

I began frantically looking through my Week-at-a-Glance to see if I had written down Woody Allen's phone number. I was afraid it was only a fantasy.

But, sure enough, I found his phone number in my Week-at-a-Glance and called him, and he answered the phone himself! When they heard me say, "Hi, Woody," two of the office workers squeezed up next to me so they could take in my every word. Although they were breathing down my neck, they were silent, so they didn't disturb me too much. Meanwhile, I was feeling exhilarated about talking with Woody. I was eager to get to know him better.

At first, Woody was warm and friendly to me in our conversation. But then something happened. It was subtle, but it was there: he became a little condescending and distant, and a little bit whiny. I didn't want this to happen; I didn't want him to be this way. I wanted Woody to be the deep, together person I imagined him to be.

I became even warmer and friendlier on the phone. I thought I would pull Woody out of his bad mood. I thought that by showing him I respected him, it would take away whatever defensive feelings were making him act the way he was acting. But it didn't work.

I then became almost pleading, not in the words I said, but with the tone of my voice. My words continued to discuss the mundane topic we were discussing—scheduling an appointment, for what I don't know—but the quality of my voice was pleading: "Please, Woody, don't be this way. Be the person you were before, or be the person I thought you were."

The phone call and the dream both ended at this point, with my disappointment.

Meg Davis's real-life story from Michael's Pub could be considered a trivial and egocentric anecdote were it not for its ring of familiarity. Several men and women who've had occasion to meet Allen, even if briefly, have commented on his apparent impatience with people who ingratiate themselves with him in any way. Any compliment for Allen seems to exceed the limits of acceptable conversation. One dreamer began a real-life chance encounter with Woody Allen in an acceptable manner. She saw him walking alone near an outdoor café in Los Angeles.

"I approached him, tapped him on the shoulder and

said: 'Excuse me. You look very familiar. Did you go to Orange County High School?'

"Woody turned around. And with a smile he replied:
'No. But you and I did have a passionate love affair one sum-
mer.' "

But then she erred.

"Then I said: 'I've always admired your work.' And
Woody withdrew. He didn't want to have any more to do
with me after that."

Many of Allen's fans felt he had been disloyal to them in
*Stardust Memories*. A number of film critics also were out-
raged by the movie. Pauline Kael wrote in *The New Yorker:*
"In *Stardust Memories*, Woody Allen degrades the people
who respond to his work and presents himself as their vic-
tim. . . . People whose attitudes, viewed differently, might
seem friendly or, at worst, over-enthusiastic and excited are
turned into morons."

Andrew Sarris in *The Village Voice* wrote: "*Stardust
Memories* is the most mean-spirited and misanthropic film I
have seen in years and years from anyone anywhere."

A *Washington Post* article by Gary Arnold read:
"There's no satiric distancing to soften or contradict the impression of fundamental distaste."

And David Denby in *New York* said: "*Stardust Memories*
is a poisonously bad movie—incoherent, madly self-impor-
tant, often boring—and the strongest, most sustained emotion in it is disgust for other people. That the emotion so
clearly comes out of Woody's disgust for himself only makes
it that much more depressing."

Why an uproar over *Stardust Memories?* Allen has
mocked pretentious, shallow, mean and mindless people in
all of his films—to the delight of fans and critics—and has
certainly expressed his disdain for pushy strangers, fans or
otherwise. Is the difference in attitude between *Stardust* and
Allen's previous films just one of degree? Many would argue

that it's not. Whereas in earlier Allen films, people were ridiculed for their lack of independent thinking and their lack of integrity, in *Stardust* people seem to be scorned for being dumb and ugly.

"Good people are rare—it's really true," Woody Allen said solemnly in the 1974 Probst interview. His statement in itself is not necessarily misanthropic. Indeed, his facial expression seemed to show more disappointment than distaste as he made this observation. It is possible that what we observe in *Stardust* is the artist's avowed anhedonia rather than misanthropy. The anhedonia prevents Allen from being able to focus on, delight in and retain pleasure from those rare "good people" he refers to. Hence the void that perhaps leaves him sometimes with only a sense of being surrounded and victimized by his abounding public of ordinary people. The distinction between misanthropy and anhedonia is relevant to the artist's motivation, where the issue becomes whether Allen's apparent contempt for people originates out of self-contempt or out of emptiness.

What does the filmmaker say? In an interview with Charles Champlin in the Los Angeles *Times*, Allen says of *Stardust Memories*: "It's about a malaise: the malaise of a man with no spiritual center, no spiritual connection. . . . My interest isn't in losers or the downtrodden. It's the problem of spiritual emptiness." In this regard, then, with *Stardust*, Allen finally got to make his *Anhedonia*, the movie that had previously been transformed into the Oscar-winning *Annie Hall*.

Nevertheless, the filmmaker does demonstrate typical symptoms of self-contempt in real life by his consistent refusal to accept personal compliments, by his difficulty in maintaining eye contact during a conversation and by his infamous limp handshake. The message Allen sends out is as much "I'm not worthy of being touched" as it is "Don't touch me." In his "Selections from the Allen Notebooks," he writes,

"Today I saw a red-and-yellow sunset and thought, How insignificant I am! Of course, I thought that yesterday, too, and it rained. I was overcome with self-loathing and contemplated suicide again—this time by inhaling next to an insurance salesman."

One can only speculate as to why Woody Allen could feel so unworthy. However, Allen tells us consistently in his films that he feels a responsibility to humanity:

> I can't enjoy anything unless I . . . unless everybody is. I—you know, if one guy is starving someplace, that's . . . you know, I-I . . . it puts a crimp in my evening.
>
> —Alvy Singer in *Annie Hall*

> Shouldn't I stop making movies and do something that counts, like being a missionary or helping the blind?
>
> —Sandy Bates in *Stardust Memories*

We're so used to laughing at those lines in their given cinematic contexts that we may be missing their verity. In an interview with Frank Rich in 1979, Woody Allen said: "I have talked seriously with my friends about giving 75% of all my possessions to charity and living in much more modest circumstances. I've rationalized my way out of it so far."

Only Woody Allen can know how far he is from living up to his own standards, how much his life-style represents or contradicts his values and how much effort he puts into becoming the person he believes he should be. One can be spiritually empty without experiencing self-contempt, but to be poignantly aware of the emptiness and to have at least glimpses of the possibility of spiritual connections—without striving for them—could constitute an unacceptable conflict for a man who values his own integrity, as Woody Allen does.

# Compassion

The "contempt" dreams about Woody Allen are more than counterbalanced by those in which Dream Woody is kind, giving and magnanimous.

●

**FARREL DONOVAN,** the tall biographer whose dream about Woody Allen's outstanding sexuality was described earlier, has been remembering and attending to his dreams since he was thirteen; he was that young when he first read Freud's treatise on interpretation. He considers the following dream, which he had on a May night in 1979, to be one of his most interesting dreams.

## THE BIG MOMENT

I went to work as a mailroom boy for a film animation and special-effects company. I was a writer, but I was broke, and so I took this job where I was in the lowest position of the twenty or thirty people working there. I didn't tell them I was a writer. I just said I needed a job, and I got the job as mailroom boy.

The company was in a brownstone in the thirties on the East Side of Manhattan. The bottom floor of the company was a huge living room with sofas and chairs. The individual offices were off to the side of this very large room. It didn't look like a place of business.

I learned that this film organization had been a small, struggling company for a while, until they were lucky enough to get Woody Allen as a client. The company did both the titles and whatever special effects there were for *Manhattan*.

I was excited to learn that Allen was a client of this firm and I asked some of the staff what he was like to work with. "Well, he's very easy to work with, but then we rarely see him," I was told. "You know, we operate through memoranda and through phone calls, and we send things back and forth by messenger, but in fact, he's never even been to this place. It may be that the owner has met him once, but Woody Allen has never come here himself."

"But wouldn't it be interesting if he did come here and we all got a chance to meet him?" I said, excited at the prospect of that actually happening.

Each morning I went in to the company and wrapped packages, sorted mail and did whatever routine work was needed along those lines. Then, one day during lunch hour, something special happened.

This particular day most of the staff had gone out to eat. There was the receptionist who answered the phones, myself and perhaps two or three people left in the entire building. I was seated in the main room eating my lunch when I saw a taxicab drive up to the entrance of the building. It was obvious to me that the people were coming into our building so I went out to greet the taxi.

A little boy jumped out of the cab. He was about seven or eight years old, and he was an exact replica of Woody Allen. He wore horn-rimmed glasses and he had a large nose, and he was just like a seven-year-old Woody Allen.

"Wow!" I exclaimed. "You *must* be Woody Allen's son!"

"Yeah, I am," he answered without smiling, and then, indicating the package he was carrying, he added: "I have to deliver this to your company."

I was so engrossed in talking with this boy that I didn't notice there were other people in the cab. I was asking him questions like "How is your father?" and "Did you have anything to do with the film?'' and "Did you help your father?'' I was interested in engaging the kid, but I wasn't patronizing. I could see he was highly intelligent.

At some point, I glanced over at the cab, and there was Allen, sitting in the taxi, watching all of this—me trying to engage his son! There were four or five other people in the taxi, too, movie kind of people, starlets—girls in tight pants, with attractive hair.

Allen had a slight smile on his face as he watched me trying to engage his son. "Do you work here?'' he asked me. And I said, "Yes, I work in the mailroom.'' And he immediately replied: "You know, I've never been in there; I think I'd like to go in and see how they operate.''

The minute Allen said this I realized he was coming inside not because he wanted to see the inside of the place; after all, he hadn't seen it in all of the time that the company was doing the special effects for *Manhattan*. Rather, he was doing it because he liked me. And he liked me because I was engaging his son without being patronizing to the child.

I ran inside first as Woody and the other people were getting out of the taxi. "You're not going to believe this, Woody Allen's coming in!'' I shouted.

"You'd better call the president of the company. Find out where he's having lunch and call him there; he'll probably want to come right back; this might be good for business!'' I ordered. And the other staff members were looking at me oddly, thinking, "What is this mailroom boy doing ordering people around as though he's the executive of a company?'' But I went on, "Go get champagne, and get some clean glasses out!''

Woody Allen and his whole retinue came inside now. One of the staff came over with the glasses and poured champagne. People were milling about, and things were working out well. The room itself was an attractive place for a gathering.

There was one especially long sofa in the room, and I sat on one end of it. Allen walked over, looked around and then sat on the

other end of the sofa. Again I said to myself: "He could have sat anywhere else in the room. But this is a signal to engage me, to let me know that he wants further communication."

"Are you sure you're just a mailroom boy? What do you do otherwise?" were his first questions to me.

"Well, as a matter of fact, I'm a writer—but I don't tell anyone," I was glad to have the opportunity to tell him.

Then I thought, "This could be my great opportunity! I've always wanted to write a screenplay. And here I am talking to the most famous director in the United States. I could both make myself a small fortune and also write my screenplay at last, if I get this man's attention. This is a big moment in my life!"

I then became terribly frightened by what was happening. I said to myself: "If I say the right thing, and he becomes interested in me, he'll hire me to write a screenplay. And if I say the wrong thing, I blow it." It was all black and white in my mind.

Now, I'm not a very humorous person: I don't crack jokes, ordinarily. I'm not a wit. Yet I suddenly started to become very witty as I talked to Allen. And the humor came easily to me. I was being witty and he was cracking up! He was really laughing!

Allen thought I was so funny that he turned to the other people in the room and said: "Hey, everybody—quiet down! Listen to him; this guy is very funny!"

Allen had everybody listen to me, and I kept spouting off these lines one after another, and they were all extremely witty.

Then, right in the middle of all this, I suddenly stood up, and Allen stood up. I went over to him and I picked him up in my arms, like you would pick up a child. I wanted to be affectionate to him, but instead of kissing him or showing affection in some other way, I picked him up.

He put his arm around my shoulder for additional support, and I held him like that. And he looked at me and then I thought: "My God, what am I doing? What a stupid, ridiculous thing I am doing! Why am I doing this?"

I was extremely upset, but I just stood there, holding Woody Allen in my arms. And I thought, "This man, because he is small, probably has a terrible height complex that he's been trying to get over all of his life, and here I do the one thing that someone shouldn't do to him, which is to call attention to his height."

I didn't know what to do. I looked at Woody again—I felt terribly helpless—and I said, "I'm blowing it, aren't I?"

Allen didn't say anything at all. There was total silence in the room now. But I knew by the look in Allen's eyes that he knew that I was concerned, upset and embarrassed. And then I could tell that, for that reason, he was relaxing, and he wasn't down on me, after all. He realized that I was aware I had made a tremendous blunder, and because I was aware, it was all right with him.

He showed me that he was a big man. He was small physically, but he was a big man. He understood me, and was saying to me, without words, "I realize you only got overexcited because this is such a big moment in your life."

I put him down then, and we both sat back down on the sofa. We continued to talk about my writing career, and about my interests, more quietly now, and here my dream faded off.

Farrel says he is "always going through a career confrontation and feeling insecure about it. . . . Am I doing the right thing? I always think I'm going to write a screenplay, and I haven't. At the age of forty-five it's unlikely that I'm going to write a screenplay. But I might . . . probably not." He thinks this dream manifests "a self-destructive urge: like I was trying to blow it." Thanks to Dream Woody's magnanimity, the dream still ends on a note of optimism.

Farrel's preoccupation with Woody Allen's size is apparent in both of his dreams, as well as in his gross miscalculation of real-life Allen's height when he spotted him on a Manhattan street. Farrel was sure that Allen was just five feet tall, whereas, in fact, he is five feet six inches tall. The difference in size may relate to Farrel's competitiveness with

Allen. Having grown up to be proud of his stature, it's possible that Farrel finds it confusing, as though unfair, that "this scrawny little guy" has it all.

•

**LILLY O'LEARY** asked that I say only that she is a young woman from Manhattan. Lilly had the following dream in June 1980.

—————————— **TASTEFUL LIVING** ——————————

I was sitting on the floor in a hallway in Woody's apartment. Woody and I were making idle chatter.

The entire time Woody and I were talking there were two women passing back and forth in the hallway. They lived in another apartment in the building and were moving furniture through Woody's hallway on the way to their own apartment.

The two women were bizarre characters to be seen here. The older woman was divorced and probably an alcoholic. I thought even the daughter might be an alcoholic. Their bodies were somewhat misshapen and their hard lives showed in their faces. They weren't tasteful people and I was surprised that they lived here in Woody Allen's building.

The two women were loud but Woody was nonchalant about them. The daughter stopped by us for a moment and showed Woody some delicate paper art objects. And Woody told her he really liked them.

Near us was a closed door. After chatting with me a few minutes, Woody opened the door and asked me if I would like to go in. I looked through the doorway and saw that it was his bedroom—a beautiful white room with a white bed in it.

The bedroom was compelling. I could sense a whole lot of goodness in the room. It was as though there was a force that wanted me to enter. Still, there was another force that told me I shouldn't.

I feared that I might be overwhelmed if I entered the room, that entering the room would insinuate a connection between Woody and myself. And this connection, as wonderful as it might be, would mean leaving the life I had—my husband, whom I love—and moving on to a life that I didn't know anything at all about.

I made a quick compromise. I knew there was a bathroom in the bedroom and I decided to enter Woody's bedroom only on the pretext that I wanted to use the bathroom.

When I came out of the bathroom Woody was waiting for me. "I want to show you something," he said.

I went with Woody down a narrow white hallway. The hallway floor was covered with shallow blue water that glistened with the light streaming in through the windows lining one wall. It was more than beautiful. As the sun hit the water the experience was dazzling.

We continued down this long narrow hallway and made a turn at its end. And right there was a beautiful blue swimming pool! And in the pool was an enclosed motorboat. The boat was rather large with two windows on top.

I was taken aback. I had never seen anything so brilliant. Woody and I stood by the pool and I went on and on about how astonishing and wonderful this sight was. But Woody remained nonchalant. He acknowledged that it was wonderful, but he didn't think it was important.

I remembered the way Woody had related to the two rather tasteless women. And I was impressed that Woody was surrounded by so much beauty—and even seemed to portray beauty himself—but at the same time was a very compassionate person.

Lilly's bright dream is one of only three color dreams she has ever had. "It was magical," says Lilly of her dream. "It seemed sexual because it was so sensual. And it was really like nothing I had ever experienced in anyone before. It seemed like a lot of goodness, a whole lot of goodness. Like something I could really trust."

Dream Woody is Lilly's guide throughout the dream. As in other dreams, he seems to be her magical traveling companion. He first opens the door to his pure, white bedroom, offering her its compelling "goodness," and he then leads her down the narrow white hallway. The shallow water in the hall, illuminated by light and culminating in a swimming pool, symbolizes progression into the unconscious, a search for spiritual meaning. The boat waiting in the pool may be a vehicle for that search. Like Dream Woody's bedroom, the boat represents an invitation: potential waiting to be actualized. There are even two windows so Lilly and Dream Woody can be fully aware of their journey as they make it.

In a sense Lilly's dream resembles Bill Monte's dream (in which Dream Woody moves from a proper British room to a rowdy Western bar). In Bill's dream, Dream Woody's talent is confirmed by a break with the past (telling off his girlfriend). In Lilly's dream she fears following Dream Woody will mean she'll have to break with the past, in particular with her husband. Both dreams have disfigured women who are part of Dream Woody's world. In Lilly's dream she is impressed that Dream Woody is able to recognize—or, maybe, elicit—beauty from one of the two unfortunate women (who shows him some delicate paper art objects). However, Lilly's dream has a clarity and directedness as well as a life-affirming quality that Bill's dream lacks, suggesting she is closer than Bill to fulfilling some potential or obtaining an important insight.

•

**JEANNIE EUBANK** is a college student who grew up in a strict, atheistic household. Jeannie has vivid memories of worrying about death and the universe while walking to first grade. She also recalls a sad period of her life when she was a patient in a psychiatric institution. Woody Allen was the only person she could think of at that time who shared her feelings about life. The thought that there was another person who could understand her, even though she had never met him, was significant in speeding her recovery.

Jeannie identified with the sense of despair she found in Allen's work. And she noted that Allen dealt with his despair with humor. When she began to allow her own sense of humor to surface more in her awareness, she was gradually able to manage her despair. She eventually overcame the depression that had accompanied the despair and led to her hospitalization.

The dream below, from October 1979, portrays the sanctum Woody provided for Jeannie. She had this dream not long after being introduced to Woody Allen in real life.

### FIFTH AVENUE HOSTEL

I had come from the suburbs into New York City. As night grew near, I realized I needed a place to stay. Fortunately I remembered that Woody Allen used his apartment as a youth hostel.

Woody's apartment was a multipurpose shelter. It wasn't necessarily just a place to sleep. You could come there if you needed a cup of coffee or just some temporary refuge.

When I arrived at Woody's hostel I saw that it was larger than I had expected. And it was filled with girls and young women. The women had backpacks and thongs and they were all sitting around drinking coffee.

I made myself at home in Woody's shelter. I felt so relaxed there that I stayed for several days.

•

**KAREN BOCCANA** is a stand-up comic who thinks of Woody Allen as her "never-present mentor." She's been a

Woody Allen fan since she was twelve years old, when she first saw him on the Jack Paar show and thought he was a funny, sexy man with sharp perception.

Karen has resisted lowering her standards of taste for the material she writes and performs, though she has been told that doing so would broaden the appeal of her act. She doesn't always find it easy to stick to her standards. The competition in her field makes it tempting to seek easier laughs. She says she resists the temptation by reminding herself that Woody Allen has stuck with his own material, rather than following other people's standards. Karen has had the following dream twice.

--- **SELSKAP ET** ---

I was at a party in a beach house on Fire Island. White-painted flowers and lots of bold green plants decorated the house. I was wearing a long, pale party dress.

I saw Woody Allen. He had on a white shirt and beige pants. And like me, he was wearing glasses. I really wanted to speak to him.

I knew I had to say the thing that was straight from my heart, so I approached Woody and said: "I don't even know what to say to you."

Woody laughed and with great charm put me at ease. He made me know that he liked me and was impressed with me.

I saw Liv Ullmann, dressed in lavender, across the room. I felt so at ease after my experience with Woody that I approached Liv and began to chat with her in Norwegian.

Karen says her dream "was telling me to hold out for the things I believe in. When I get depressed, I remember this dream."

●

**SAMUEL GREENBAUM** is an assistant publicist. Allen has been an inspiration to him as a writer since his college years of communications study in Boston.

Samuel once published an article in a New Jersey newspaper describing the time he *almost* met Woody Allen in Ocean Grove, New Jersey, where the filmmaker was on location. "Those short seconds when he passed me were unfair. . . . As he approached, everything I'd ever imagined saying to him was useless. Watching him race directly before me, I was stunned. The moment—one I'd spent years waiting for—had found me, when I was suddenly confronted with the conundrum 'What do you say to Woody Allen?' "

Samuel's question came up time and again from the men and women interviewed for this book, but usually only in their dreams. Samuel had five dreams about Allen in the years following their near-meeting in November 1979. In each of them, Dream Woody generously resolved the conundrum.

─────── **ON MEETING WOODY, VERSION ONE** ───────

My father and I went to Ocean Grove. As we walked near the beach we ran into Woody Allen. Woody reached out and shook my hand; he said he liked the story I had written about him.

I felt good standing there with my father and Woody Allen, my father figure. They were both important men in my life.

After complimenting me on my article, Woody very spontaneously hugged me! "I want you to come and work for me," he said. "I'd like for you to work sound."

The hug and the offer were both surprises.

Dream Woody made things easy for Samuel by taking the initiative and reaching out to him in perfect wish fulfillment. Samuel's matter-of-fact referral to Dream Woody as "my father figure" reflects a common feeling among the men and women interviewed.

•

**SAMUEL GREENBAUM** was surprised again in his second dream about Woody Allen.

_____ ON MEETING WOODY, VERSION TWO _____

I was in the Convention Hall arcade in Asbury Park when who should I spot but Woody Allen! I was nervous but I managed to murmur "Hello" as I rushed past him.

Woody turned all the way around to catch my attention and stop me, since I had whizzed past him. "Hello," he said.

I was really surprised.

# The Grim Psyche

In his short story "My Speech to the Graduates," Allen
writes:

More than any other time in history, mankind faces a cross-
roads. One path leads to despair and utter hopelessness. The
other, to total extinction. Let us pray we have the wisdom to
choose correctly. I speak, by the way, not with any sense of futility,
but with a panicky conviction of the absolute meaninglessness of
existence which could easily be misinterpreted as pessimism. It is
not. It is merely a healthy concern for the predicament of modern
man. (Modern man is here defined as any person born after
Nietzsche's edict that "God is dead," but before the hit recording
"I Wanna Hold Your Hand.")

Fans' identification with Woody Allen is often on either
a philosophical or a spiritual level. They see in the artist an
involvement with the same moral turning points, dilemmas
and crises that affect their own lives. Some of the dreamers
see Allen as a guide, but a few of them expressed frustration
at Allen's sluggish progress in developing his inner world. In
Joy Mahanes's words: "He seems to see things so clearly and
yet he's still blocked."

Most of the dreamers see themselves neither as leaders
nor as followers of Woody Allen in moral or spiritual pur-
suits, but as peers in a search for greater development in
these areas. Their involvement with Allen's work is a part of
their struggle to confront their own psyches. It follows, then,
that water is the most common symbol in this collection of

dreams. As a dream symbol, water often represents contact with one's unconscious, or renewal through making peace within one's inner world. The ocean, rivers and fountains, as well as other symbols of the unconscious—caves, tunnels and other dark, secluded places—are especially prevalent in the dreams that follow.

•

HARRY STEINBERG is a thirty-eight-year-old vocational counselor who says Woody Allen inspires him to be more adventurous. Harry has seen Allen in person once, on a Saturday afternoon in 1977, walking on Madison Avenue, wearing his familiar army coat and hat. He had the dream below in 1974, just after he had begun practicing diaphragmatic breathing as a way of falling asleep restfully.

––––––––––––––––––– BEACH BALL –––––––––––––––––––

It was early morning. Woody and I were playing volleyball on the beach. It was a strange and delightful experience. I was joyful, and my body felt light and buoyant.

Woody and I were on opposite sides of the net. There were a lot of other people playing volleyball with us. I'd never seen these other men and women.

As we played, the other players would slowly disappear and there would only be Woody and me for a while. Then, just as unobtrusively, other new players would come into the game. It was an exhaustive and competitive game that went on and on. But through it all, Woody's presence enabled me to feel light and playful.

Woody's clothes changed spontaneously just as the people playing changed. Woody was wearing a shirt and shorts at first, but his shorts kept changing into other shorts. And then there was one vivid moment when Woody was wearing a fisherman's long raincoat and a fisherman's tucked-up hat. Then back to shorts.

Woody was light and graceful as he tapped and spiked the ball, and his face manifested delight and confusion. I experienced his lightness as an invitation to myself to shift gears, change lenses and be surreal.

I woke up feeling light and buoyant.

Harry says his dream encouraged him to see things in a surreal way, to be able to move more easily back and forth between an active state and a passive one and to integrate his dream life and his waking life. Dream Woody's frequent, spontaneous clothes changes suggest that change can be a fluid, natural part of life. The strangers, as well as the nearness to water, symbolize the unconscious. Harry's dream is reassuring him in suggesting that reaching deeper into his unconscious can be exhausting without being painful.

•

JEANNIE EUBANK, who previously found refuge in Dream Woody's youth hostel, was comforted by him again in the next dream.

_____ SO NEAR AND YET SO FAR _____

Woody and I were swimming together in the ocean. Not out to sea, but parallel to the beach. We were swimming through some very rough waters and I could feel myself searching—searching as I swam.

At the same time I was swimming in the ocean with Woody, I could see Woody on the beach, playing tennis with another person! I had a clear vision of him playing tennis with someone else, while at the same time he was clearly there with me, swimming and searching.

Swimming and being immersed in water symbolize renewal and hope for Jeannie in this dream and in several of her other dreams. She had this dream as she was in the process of coming out of her depression and gaining a sense of control over her life. An especially healthy aspect of this dream is that Jeannie is learning in it to be comforted by Dream Woody, to feel his presence, even when she can see that he is somewhere else. Thus, she is beginning to internalize the hope that Woody Allen has offered her, rather than needing to embody it in his physical presence.

•

**MAX SPARKS** is a thirty-three-year-old gas station attendant who grew up in Jerusalem and in 1974 moved to "the greatest city in the world, New York." Max enjoys Allen's "uniqueness, the fact that you can never predict what he's going to do next, and that he's simple and normal, not a snob," most of all. Max began dreaming about Allen in 1973, while he was still living in Israel. His dreams about the filmmaker are all adventures in which Dream Woody often protects him, as he does in the following dream from 1978.

### THE PROMISED LAND

The road was gray and still. There was nothing moving, except, way in the distance, a lone hitchhiker. As I got closer I could see it was a man. I slowed down my car, preparing to stop for him, but the man disappeared. So I went on my way and ended up at Jones Beach.

I hadn't been in the water long at all before the shark appeared—a giant shark—and he immediately started after me! But I barely had time to be terrified before I was saved. It was Woody Allen to my rescue! There he was, swimming toward me and the shark. He looked just like he looks in the movies: a man who never combs his hair. Woody grabbed hold of the shark and then yelled to me to grab hold of *him.* So I held on to Woody and he held on to the shark, and the shark led us to shore—not back to Jones Beach, but to another shore. The shore was far away, but the ride there was an adventure. And when we arrived, we saw that we'd come to a beautiful land, a really beautiful land.

Here again, it is hope or salvation that Max's favorite New York Jew helps him to find. The shark at first seems to be a terrifying aspect of the unconscious, threatening to devour Max. With Dream Woody's intervention it becomes a constructive force, leading Max and Dream Woody to a higher state of awareness. Woody Allen's art serves much the same purpose for his audience. The characters Woody Allen portrays in his films, like Allen himself, reveal remarkable anxiety. The face we see on the screen is often angst-struck. But Woody Allen's anxiety is not debilitating. His humor with its acute perception elevates the anxiety to a higher level of consciousness—for himself and for his audience.

•

CLIFF CUDAHEY is a fifty-two-year-old artist who lives in Los Angeles with his wife and three daughters. Cliff thinks Allen is unique in the way he explores hypocrisy in the world. He admires the filmmaker for "doing with his art what most people would do through vindictiveness." He sees Allen as "an archetypical character who is living the statement of what art is." Cliff is currently writing three novels and four screenplays and painting pictures when he is not at the typewriter. His dream is from 1977.

_____ SAFE WITH WOODY _____

I was on a boat with five women: my three daughters, my present wife and a woman in black who was dressed to the nines and saying silly profound things. Woody Allen came rushing up to us and began dispensing orders.

"We've got to do this and we've got to do that," Woody told us. He then led us through the ship, which was a myriad of stairways and ballrooms. The six of us moved together as though we were one. There was a desperation to our efforts. And Woody was nervous. But my women and I had complete confidence in him. We were with Woody Allen and everything was going to be fine as long as we stayed with him.

For Cliff this dream reinforced his belief that living with confusion is okay, if there is meaning to the experience. Dream Woody is a leader in the search for meaning, symbolized by the confusing ocean voyage of Cliff's dream.

•

HUGH FRANK is a thirty-year-old poet who considers himself to be a Woody Allen lookalike. In 1976 he tried to get a job as a stand-in for Allen. The son of a rabbi, with an extensive Judaic background, Hugh is a Ph.D. candidate but considers himself to be an anti-intellectual. Hugh believes "there is an illness in the New York Jew whereby something spiritual has become smug and self-contained." As much as he admires Allen's talent, he sometimes almost hates him for his failure to confront this illness. "Why couldn't he have taken that talent and applied it in another way?"

Hugh's assessment bears a lot in common with that of the character Isaac in *Manhattan*, who wrote of himself: " 'He adored New York City. To him, it was a metaphor for the decay of contemporary culture. The same lack of individual integrity to cause so many people to take the easy way out . . . was rapidly turning the town of his dreams in—' No, it's gonna be too preachy." Hugh has conveyed his philosophical concerns to Allen both in the following 1978 dream and in a letter he sent to Allen the day afterward.

─────────── **BREAKTHROUGH** ───────────

I was at Woody's, an informal, messy place. Woody and I were sitting on the floor.

Woody, like myself, was wearing a dark-green and brown-flannel early-Woody shirt. We were dressed alike because our identities kept merging.

As I sat there talking to Woody, sometimes I would find I was alone, just talking to myself. And at other times I was Woody talking either to himself or to me.

There was an urgency to my communication with Woody. And an enormous satisfaction that Woody accepted my point of view.

By getting through to Woody I was correcting a major theological and philosophical wrong in the world among all Jews and all people—the whole New York syndrome.

For Hugh, Woody Allen is the quintessential New York Jew, and the New York Jew symbolizes a particular corruption of spirituality. His wish-fulfilling dream helped him to feel more at peace and deepened his sense of intimacy with Allen. Still, his frustration at the way Allen uses his potential continues to flare up now and then, as does his anguish over "the whole New York syndrome."

●

**DOROTHY NEER** is a waitress at the Source Restaurant, the L.A. health-food restaurant where Alvy and Annie's parting scene in *Annie Hall* was shot. Dorothy is a single parent who grew up in Las Vegas and whose favorite Woody Allen movie is *Take the Money and Run.* Of Allen, she says, "God bless him for his search for immortality, his attitudes about life and for *Without Feathers.*" Dorothy rarely remembers dreams but when she does they're usually about Allen.

### THE CARNIVAL

I was at a carnival and Woody Allen was in a sideshow. He was trying to get someone from the crowd of people watching to volunteer to stab him with a knife. "C'mon," he called, but no one volunteered. So Woody picked me! There I was, wearing a see-through white skirt with multicolored pajama bottoms on, and Woody picked me to come up and stab him! Oh well, I figured my clothes were pretty much like his—comfortable, but awful and unconventional.

He kept on daring someone to kill him. Then he turned to me again. "C'mon!" he said. So I did it. I went at him with the knife and hit him in the chest and it was one of those collapsible knives!

The crowd was angry and began to chase him. He grabbed me by the hand and we ran together. We ran home to my house, since I live here. Bob was there. I introduced Woody and Bob, and Bob said Woody could stay, but he'd have to sleep on the floor with the cat. We don't have a cat! I got the idea Bob didn't like Woody. I gave Woody a blanket, and we all prepared for bed.

Then, later in the evening, Woody and I got up, found my bikes, and went cycling on the beach as the sun set beside us.

Dorothy says that in her dream Woody chose her to share the experience of confronting death with him, and because of that, she knew she could trust him completely. The outfit Dorothy is wearing—the see-through white skirt with multicolored pajama bottoms—evokes the image of women in old Indian miniatures, appropriate symbolism since Indians participate in death rituals more than do Westerners. Dorothy's man's fear of her involvement with Dream Woody is seen in the dream's symbolism, too: in Egyptian mythology a cat is the guardian of marriage.

•

CHRISTOPHER SALCEDO is a nineteen-year-old Cuban film student who plays the saxophone. Christopher thinks Allen is the most creative person he's ever seen on screen. He's especially impressed with the way Allen "relates everything to sex!" Christopher had the following dream while rehearsing for the role of Death in a 1979 university production of *Death Knocks,* Woody Allen's one-act play.

---

### IDENTITY CRISIS

I was walking through an exceptionally long, dark tunnel. I had barely entered the tunnel when large, menacing hands began to reach out from the wall. The hands were in back of me and all along the tunnel wall on the right of me. And they were trying to get me.

I could not turn back. I could only move forward and to the left.

It was a harrowing experience. I continued to make my way forward, keeping as close to the left wall as possible and managing somehow to keep those awful hands from touching me.

I finally approached the end of the tunnel. A mirror with light emanating from it was at the tunnel's mouth.

I looked into the mirror and saw the reflection of Death. But the face of Death was Woody Allen's rather than my own.

In his dream Christopher's identity, like Hugh Frank's, merged with Dream Woody's, in this case reflecting his waking-life identification with Allen's obsession with death. It is an obsession that was probably intensified for Christopher by his playing Death in Allen's play. The end of Christopher's dream is similar to the passage from *Death Knocks* in which Nat notices Death's resemblance to him and says to Death, "I said you looked like me. It's like a reflection." Later, in describing Death to his wife, Nat adds: "But, Moe, he's such a *schlep!*"

The long, dark tunnel in Christopher's dream represents the darkness, seclusion and mystery of the unconscious, and moving to the left also symbolizes moving toward the unconscious side of experience. The menacing hands reaching out for Christopher seem, even more than the shark in Max

Sparks's dream, to represent terrifying aspects of the unconscious. The ending is ambiguous. Christopher approaches the tunnel's end and it seems that he's going to be successful in avoiding engulfment by the frightening elements of his unconscious; still, when he tries to confront awareness of his death head on, it's Woody's reflection rather than his own that is returned to him. The dream's ambiguous ending suggests that Christopher still needs his identification with Allen to help in probing his unconscious. The ending of Christopher's dream also recalls an early Allen stand-up routine in which he describes his life flashing before his eyes as the Ku Klux Klan prepares to hang him:

And suddenly my whole life passed before my eyes. I saw myself as a kid again in Kansas going to school, swimmin' at the swimmin' hole and fishin' and fryin' up a mess o' catfish; goin' down to the general store and getting a piece a' gingham for Emmie Lou. And I realize it's not *my* life!

•

**JOE MOSES** is a twenty-nine-year-old diamond sorter who recently left New York City to return to San Francisco, where he grew up. Joe, whose favorite Woody Allen film is *Play It Again, Sam,* thinks Allen "represents the sixties in his striving for something intelligent." Joe was in the process of deciding whether to leave his rabbinical studies at the time of the following dream in January 1980.

### —————— WOODY AND/OR MY RABBI ——————

I went to my rabbi's house. I entered through the front door and walked through the foyer.

My rabbi and Woody Allen were together at my rabbi's desk. An open Talmud was before them.

I felt like the odd man out as I approached Woody and my

rabbi. I was concerned that I was interrupting something important.

It seemed that these two men represented the two different worlds I was conflicted about: the two different worlds I wanted.

And then I had another thought: "Maybe it's the same world."

Joe's dream clarified the issues he was struggling with at the time, and he realized afterward that one's occupation isn't all one is, that one doesn't have to be a rabbi to lead a spiritual life.

"My real obsessions are religious," Woody Allen said in a 1979 interview with Frank Rich. "They have to do with the meaning of life. . . . I spend a lot of time face to face with my own mortality." Allen's obsession with his mortality prompted Andrew Sarris to remark in the *Village Voice* (October 1–7, 1980) that, "The fact that one remains mortal even as one rises into a higher tax bracket hardly calls for the invocation of Schopenhauer." It is true, as Sarris implies, that preoccupation with one's death can stem from shallow origins, such as narcissism, or frustration in realizing goals (fear of dying unfulfilled). Allen himself made this point in *Manhattan*. A passage from the book that Ike's ex-wife, Jill, had written about their relationship says of him: "He was given to fits of rage, Jewish, liberal paranoia, male chauvinism, self-righteous misanthropy, and nihilistic moods of despair. He had complaints about life but never any solutions. . . . He longed to be an artist but balked at the necessary sacrifices. In his most private moments, he spoke of his fear of death, which he elevated to tragic heights when, in fact, it was mere narcissism." (As always, it's difficult to say anything meaningful about Allen's personality that he has not already said of himself.)

Is it narcissism that prompts Allen's death obsession? Is he really "The Shallowest Man," as described in the story of

that title? Woody Allen repeatedly condemns the shallow-
ness of our culture in his work. It is this concern that, in fact,
seems to be the primary basis for his fans' identification with
him. In *Annie Hall*, troubled over the failure of his love life,
Alvy stops a happy-looking couple and asks how they do it.
The woman replies: "Uh, I'm very shallow and empty, and I
have no ideas and nothing interesting to say." In the same
movie, Alvy also comments, "I think there's too much burden
placed on the orgasm, you know, to make up for empty areas
in life." The viewpoint Allen has presented in his work is,
of course, that our preoccupation with our daily lives is a
way of remaining unaware of grander matters, particularly
that of our mortality.

The skepticism of some critics about the depth of Allen's
religious considerations may be spurred in part by the lack of
development of these themes in his films. Death, religion and
morality are themes developed more fully in his stories,
essays and short plays, though his films are permeated with
references to them: *Love and Death* has death as a central
topic; both *Interiors* and *Stardust Memories* focus on spiritual
emptiness, and *A Midsummer Night's Sex Comedy* considers
the possibility of a spirit world. Nonetheless, as subject matter, these topics are always surpassed by human relationships.
Allen deals directly and fully with his feelings about romantic
involvements and friendships, but so far he has not really
presented his religious obsessions head on in his movies.
Clearly, however, he has revealed his deeper concerns
strongly enough for his followers to respond to them intensely. It is Allen's *struggle* to attain meaning, as much as his
wisdom itself, that fans identify with.

Woody Allen, with his poignant wisdom, sees it all: that
art is nothing next to life; that talent is luck and therefore not
something to take pride in; that all of our neurotic preoccu-
pations with careers and relationships are merely ways of
distracting ourselves from issues we're afraid to confront,

such as mortality; that intellectualism is insignificant compared to the wisdom that comes from healthy intuition; and, most important, that in the absence of meaning handed down to us by some greater force, we must each determine our own meaning by establishing a system of values on which we can base moral decisions for all of our actions.

It is ironic that the move from psychology to spirituality is what Woody Allen seems not yet to have mastered. Allen says his frame of reference is philosophical and spiritual, and we sometimes see this in the Woody Allen film persona, even if most often in self-parody as in the scene from *Manhattan* in which Yale shouts at Ike: "You think you're God!" and Ike responds: "I-I gotta model myself after someone!" Yet that persona and all the other characters in Allen's films still seem trapped in the psychological society, a society in which ego rather than character dictates behavior and where the goal of ego fulfillment has become its own limitation.

It has been said by Bruno Bettelheim that mistranslations of Freud's work into English have resulted in a general misinterpretation of the very essence of psychoanalysis, by interpreting the psyche as the mind rather than as the soul. It is that distinction—between the soul and the mind as aspects of the psyche—that Woody Allen seems to be struggling with. One thing is certain, however: Woody Allen's fans identify with his grim psyche and are eagerly awaiting its further elaboration in his art.

# CONCLUSION

CONCLUSION

# Dream Woody in a Nutshell

Here, in a nutshell, is the Woody Allen of men's and women's dreams. Like the real-life Woody but strikingly unlike the original Woody film persona, Dream Woody is a competent athlete. He is muscular, graceful and proficient at the many ball games he plays, including baseball, volleyball, paddle ball and basketball.

Dream Woody has an affinity for water. In some dreams Woody has a house on the beach. In other dreams he is visiting Fire Island or another ocean community. In one dream Woody's apartment has a large indoor swimming pool, complete with boat, and his hallway floors are covered with shallow water. In several dreams Woody is either swimming or playing ball on the beach. Still other Woody dreams take place near a fountain or river. And several dreams involve boat trips.

Real-life Woody Allen told Frank Rich for the 1979 *Time* article: "I'd rather die than live in the country." But Dream Woody lives in the country, on the beach, in Brooklyn, in a converted school bus in the mountains, above Michael's Pub and overlooking Central Park, among other places.

The Woody Allen of men's and women's dreams is, like real-life Allen, a risk-taking, persevering and fastidious artist. He also is a generous filmmaker who offers his friends opportunities to collaborate on scripts and to act and even star in films. Dream Woody is a responsive audience, too, and sometimes cracks up at the great wit of new acquaintances.

Dream Woody and his buddies are mutually supportive. Dream Woody is often fatherly and protective. But his friends, in turn, can be counted on to encourage and protect him as well. Dream Woody's relationships with his friends are intimate. He and his pal always understand where the other is coming from. And they share a common lack of interest in trivia.

Dream Woody is both friends and lovers with the women in his life. He protects and encourages them—at least, the ones he respects—just as he does his male friends. As a lover, Dream Woody is romantic and kinky. As a friend, he is quiet, understanding, respectful and easy to be with. But Dream Woody is, nonetheless, a confirmed bachelor. And he is not so considerate of women who do not intrigue him. He can be cold and callous, and he leaves some women feeling that they've been used for sex.

Dream Woody gives and takes away. He has a perverse tendency to single individuals out, flatter them or flirt with them and then abruptly reject them. He also seems to get a kick out of shocking people by doing the unexpected.

Still, Dream Woody shares and usually embodies the spiritual yearnings of his friends and acquaintances. Like them, he is constantly struggling and searching for greater contact with the unconscious, for deeper meaning in life.

Finally, Dream Woody lusts over chocolate. Éclairs, chocolate candy, fudge pastries: Dream Woody craves them all, and makes it a point, wherever he may be, to get his fix.

# Woody Allen as Symbol

Identifying with a famous person can be a way of expanding one's perspective on life. Some people go to a movie or read a book to escape from their real lives. Their identification with the hero of a film or a novel is limited to the period of time in which they suspend disbelief. Once the book or movie is over, the "identification" ends and it's back to the same real world for them. Other people, however, internalize their identification with the hero or the maker of a movie; for them, films (and art, travel and other experiences) become a part of their identities and enrich, rather than distract them from, their real lives. The "escapers"—those whose identification with a movie hero is only make-believe—also resist identifying with famous people in general. As a rule, they shun such identification because they have low self-esteem and/or do not see themselves as having the potential to transcend their environments.

In dreams one can become as intimate with the essence of a hero as is possible. Dreams also reveal the nature of one's identification with that person. The dream object may represent a neglected part of oneself that needs to be nurtured or a part of one's past self that needs to be reactivated to provide continuity in one's life. Or the person identified with may represent the self that one has not yet become but is growing toward. Woody Allen often serves this function in dreams. Carl Rogers has described in his work (in *Client-Centered Therapy*, Houghton Mifflin, 1951) how "the self that one is striving to become is always the truer self than that which

**187**

manifests itself in the present." Woody Allen as dream object frequently points the way toward this truer self of the dreamer.

Most of the dreamers identify with Woody Allen in positive ways. Dream Woody is a constructive force for them, either in the dream itself or in the effect the dream has on the dreamer after awakening. One of Dream Woody's most important functions is in giving them insights into their own personalities or situations. Sandra Pappachristau achieved a greater trust for men through her breakthrough dream in which she allowed Dream Woody to father her baby. Joe Moses's dream concerning a meeting between his rabbi and Woody Allen gave him the crucial insight that he didn't have to be a rabbi to live in the spiritual world. Scott Gunn felt more comfortable with his attraction to men after he dreamed that Woody Allen played a gay man in a movie. And even though Lyn Rubin's Dream Woody rudely rejected her (throwing up on her when she annoyed him), she learned from her dream that she needs to respect herself more. Stephen Wohl and Jason Weil each had a chance to experience Woody Allen's celebrity life-style in their dreams, and both realized that, as real-life Allen tells us, it isn't what it's cracked up to be.

These men and women were encouraged and comforted by Dream Woody. Several of them, including Alma Vesley and Max Bernstein, whose dreams depicted Woody taking risks, were reminded of the importance of seeking out challenges. Ann Weide began the film studies she had been putting off after dreaming that she and Woody collaborated on a film. Lou Finklestein found renewed energy for plugging away at his doctoral dissertation after Dream Woody assured him he was on the right track. And Karen Boccana's dream about Allen reinforced her determination to stick to her artistic standards. Many dreamers were reassured that there was someone who could understand them and, if necessary, protect them as well. Sue Greenstein, for instance, found special comfort in her Woody dream during a time when she felt she could not count on her husband for support.

A few of the men and women interviewed for this book may have used their identification with Woody Allen to destructive ends. None of the dreamers replaced their own identity with Allen's (Jason Weil as a teenager perhaps came close to doing that, but as he matured he let go of his excessive imitating of the filmmaker); however, a few of the dreamers did use their identification with the artist to justify self-limiting attitudes rather than growth-producing ones. Beanie Alston's identification with Dream Woody's condescending posture, for instance, is blatantly apparent in the words she uses to describe her dream ("Mr. Allen could tell that those *monkeys* behind the police barricade wouldn't understand what he was saying even if they heard him"), as is Stu Sanders's condescension ("I became aware that I really didn't like these people in my audience. In fact, I felt contempt for them"). Stu is aware of his inclinations toward arrogance, but Beanie, I think, has not yet seen herself as clearly as Dream Woody must have in her dream. She doesn't perceive herself as having been condescending in the dream. On the other hand, when Fred Forman *quit* identifying with Allen, after Dream Woody made him feel anonymous ("Fred is just a name I use for people I don't know"), he shut a door on his own potential for growth. By deciding that Woody Allen was inaccessible, Fred was defining his world as one with predetermined boundaries that he dare not hope to exceed.

All of these dreams can, of course, be interpreted as having significance beyond the relationship of the dreamer to Woody Allen. Joy Mahanes's and Evelyn Murphy's loneliness, Michael Klapman's and Farrel Donovan's self-doubts, and the struggle for mastery, either artistic or personal, suggested in over half of the dreams, are concerns that remain to be addressed by the dreamers, even after the insights obtained from their Woody dreams. What is significant here, however, is that it is Woody Allen who appears in these dreams to evoke such strong realizations and insights about important issues in the dreamers' lives. What is it about Woody Allen that motivates men and women to seek out higher states of awareness? What does Woody Allen symbolize for his fans?

Being true to oneself ranks high among the qualities he embodies for the men and women I interviewed for this book. As Doug Watson summarized Dream Woody, "He knew what he wanted and what he didn't want." The dreamers see Allen as a person who is intensely honest about his feelings and who admits his faults as well as his strengths. They experience his vulnerability as a strength and doing so helps them feel stronger themselves. When Allen expresses fear, the dreamers feel reassured, rather than disturbed, by his candor. "I'm scared," Dream Woody told Laurie Sweeney on their rough ocean voyage. "You're so available to me and to my feelings," she responded.

It is Allen's openness that motivates the dreamers to be more honest themselves and hence more self-accepting. And his honesty accounts at least partly for the "uniqueness" of his personality that fans describe (the more one reveals about oneself, on a genuine and emotional level, the more we are able to discern their individualism). But there's more to being unique than being revealing. Allen is also seen as an independent thinker. Evelyn Murphy described him as a person who "does not kowtow to the crowd and the mores of society," and several dreamers referred to the artist as "a maverick."

The individualism is manifested symbolically by the leadership role Dream Woody frequently plays (advising the dreamers, directing them); in the surprises Dream Woody presents to the dreamers ("'By the way,' he said. 'If you get the part, that bird is not the bird you'll be working with. . . .

This is the real bird.' Clinging to his shoulder was an eagle"); and in Dream Woody's own special way of expressing himself ("How do you take your soup?" he asked Joy Mahanes, thereby letting her know of his deep commitment to her).

Fans see Allen as a risk taker, a person who is not afraid to be different and not afraid to fail. Dream Woody takes a multitude of risks: sliding down a mattress and taking a headlong dive from a fourth-floor window ("He was determined to do something different"), saving one dreamer from a shark ("It was Woody Allen to my rescue!"), daring another dreamer to stab him with a knife (albeit a collapsible one), nonchalantly riding high across the Harlem River Bridge in a cable car and playing a homosexual role in a movie. Among the risks Allen has taken in his real life, the two that the dreamers referred to repeatedly, are his continuing experimentation in his filmmaking and, again, his willingness to reveal his vulnerability to the world at large.

The development of Allen's work has depended on perseverance as well as on experimentation. Woody Allen strongly symbolizes perseverance for the dreamers. They wake up from their Woody dreams motivated to "stick to it," "not give up" and "keep working hard and stay with where I think my center is." Dream Woody inspires his followers much as real-life Allen encourages his colleagues and friends, some of whom regret their inability to reciprocate fully. Many of the men and women I interviewed share this regret.

Referring to his childhood, Woody Allen said in an early stand-up routine, "At that age I identified with Superman. I felt Superman and I had many things in common. He used to go into telephone booths and remove his clothing all the time. And so did I." And of his adult sexuality, he observed: "I'm thin but I'm fun." Allen is a symbol of sexual lust and/or romantic idealism in about two thirds of the women's dreams. But judging from the people interviewed for this book, his significance as a sex symbol may be even greater for men than it is for women. "Woody Allen has given us new standards for male beauty," Wally Shawn said on a *Taxi* episode. In fact, Allen has set new standards for male behavior in general. He's broken the macho stereotype of masculinity, and he's helped men realize they can express their fears, admit their insecurities about women and their lack of athletic prowess and still feel good about themselves as men. Men see that women respond positively to the vulnerability of the Woody film persona and they realize they can relax and be themselves a little more without fear of seeming weak to the opposite sex.

Woody Allen is a symbol of genius, which is no surprise. Even without reflecting on the whole body of Allen's work, it's easy to appreciate this tribute. Even the broadest scenes from his comedies are bright and inspired. In her dream about meeting Woody in a car show, Libby Hendricks aptly summarized fans' appreciation of Allen's braininess when she said: "I knew I'd finally met someone who was an extension of myself: Woody was the person I would be if I could take my brain one step forward." Overall, the dreamers' waking perceptions of Allen are more concerned with his genius than are their dream experiences of him. Almost two thirds of the men and women I interviewed used the word "genius" as part of their description of the artist. But his intelligence, like his extraordinary humor, was not often a salient dream theme. The dreams were more often concerned with the feelings and perceptions that his real-life intelligence and humor convey.

Woody Allen is also seen in dreams as a man of contradictions—as both remarkably trustworthy and as hypocritical; as a man of great compassion and of formidable contempt. It is striking that in almost every case the dreamers perceive these contradictions as signs of the great complexity of Woody Allen's character (as they no doubt are), rather than as signs of ambivalence in their own perceptions of Allen. It is also worth noting that the contempt and hypocrisy are manifested more strongly in the fans' dreams than in their waking perceptions. This discrepancy may represent partly the reluctance of the men and women to consciously acknowledge these traits in their hero, and partly the fact that the image of contempt, for example, is obtained primarily through the dreamers' subliminal experiencing of Allen on screen: it is not an explicit attribute of the Woody film persona (at least not prior to *Stardust Memories*, which many of the dreams predate) and hence is not as likely to be experienced consciously as are qualities consistent with the Woody persona, such as vulnerability.

Finally, as funny as he is, Woody Allen is a symbol for the dreamers of a serious search for meaning. Dream Woody is a guide to the unconscious and a link between the material world and the spiritual world. Fans see Allen as someone who, like them, attaches supreme importance to confronting one's psyche and probing the unconscious to wherever that may lead. They feel comforted by the way Allen uses humor to deal with despair. However, it is the despair, more than the humor, that they identify with.

His fans associate integrity and a concern with moral matters with Woody Allen in their dreams as well as in their waking lives. Their expectations of him are high, and they are profoundly disappointed when he fails to live up to them. Why do Allen's attitudes and judgments have such a strong impact on these men and women? Partly because he most often expresses them through his instinctive humor. Laughter, like crying, is a primitive experience, and when Woody Allen makes a member of his audience laugh, he often is helping that person to be more in touch with his deepest self—the insight obtained while laughing is internalized. And partly, I think, we have to return to Allen's vulnerability to appreciate why his perceptions affect some people so deeply. His openness suggests awareness, which lends credibility to the ideas he expresses.

While the public image of Allen may be that of a Renaissance man, the Woody Allen who emerges from the dreams of his fans is even more like the archetypal modern man: the solitary, old-fashioned man whom Jung describes as transcending the present level of consciousness through acceptance of the unconscious, and whose higher level of consciousness "is like a burden of guilt." More than anything else, Woody Allen stands for a search for meaning in a shallow world. This archetypal search is probably the basis for the universality of Allen's appeal. Judging by the unsolicited letters and calls I have received, people all over the world are dreaming about Woody Allen.

Maybe the moon deer, with their starry wisdom and discriminating taste, were onto something.

# FILMOGRAPHY

*What's New, Pussycat?* (1965). Director: Clive Donner. Producer: Charles K. Feldman. Screenplay: Woody Allen. Photography: Jean Badal (Technicolor, Scope). Music: Burt Bacharach. Editor: Fergus McDonell. Sound: William-Robert Sivel. Art Director: Jacques Saulnier. Assistant Director: Enrico Isacco. Special Effects: Bob MacDonald. A Famous Artists Production. 120 minutes.

*What's Up, Tiger Lily?* (1966). Original version: *Kagi No Kagi* (*Key of Keys*) (Japan, 1964). Director: Senkichi Taniguchi. Script: Hideo Andro. Photography: Kazuo Yamada (Eastmancolor, Scope). Produced by Tomoyuki Tanaka for Toho. 94 minutes.

Rerelease Director: Woody Allen. Production Conception: Ben Shapiro. Editor: Richard Krown. Script and Dubbing: Woody Allen, Frank Buxton, Len Maxwell, Louise Lasser, Mickey Rose, Julie Bennett, Bryna Wilson. Music: The Lovin' Spoonful. 79 minutes.

*Casino Royale* (1967). Directors: John Huston, Kenneth Hughes, Val Guest, Robert Parrish, Joseph McGrath. Producers: Charles K. Feldman and Jerry Bresler. Screenplay: Wolf Mankowitz, John Law, Michael Sayers; suggested by the novel by Ian Fleming. Photography: Jack Hildyard (Panavision, Technicolor). Editor: Bill Lenny. Production Designer: Michael Ayringer. Special Effects: Cliff Richardson, Roy Whybrow. Music: Burt Bacharach. Titles, Montage: Richard Williams. A Famous Artists Production, released by Columbia Pictures. 131 minutes.

*Don't Drink the Water* (1969). Director: Howard Morris. Producer: Charles Joffe. Screenplay: R. S. Allen and Harvey Bullock; based upon the stageplay by Woody Allen. Photography: Harvey Genkins (Movielab, color). Music: Pat Williams. Art Director: Robert Gundlach. Editor: Ralph Rosenblum. Assistant Director: Louis Stroller, 98 minutes.

*Take the Money and Run* (1969). Director: Woody Allen. Script: Woody Allen and Mickey Rose.

Photography: Lester Shorr (Technicolor). Editing: Paul Jordan, Ron Kalish. Music: Marvin Hamlisch. Art Director: Fred Harpman. Special Effects: A. D. Flowers. Assistant Directors: Louis Stroller, Walter Hill. Produced by Charles H. Joffe for Palomar Pictures. 85 minutes.

*Bananas* (1971). Director: Woody Allen. Script: Woody Allen and Mickey Rose. Photography: Andrew M. Costikyan (Deluxe Color). Production Designer: Ed Wittstein. Music: Marvin Hamlisch. Editor: Ron Kalish. Associate Producer: Ralph Rosenblum. Assistant Director: Fred T. Gallo. Special Effects: Don B. Courtney. Produced by Jack Grossberg for Rollins and Joffe Productions. 81 minutes.

*Play It Again, Sam* (1972). Director: Herbert Ross. Production Supervisor: Roger M. Rothstein. Screenplay: Woody Allen; based on his stageplay. Photography: Owen Roizman (Technicolor). Music: Billy Goldberg. Editor: Marion Rothman. Assistant Director: William Gerrity. An Arthur P. Jacobs Production for Paramount Pictures. 84 minutes.

*Everything You Always Wanted to Know About Sex* (*but were afraid to ask*) (1972). Director: Woody Allen. Script: Woody Allen; from the book by David Reuben. Photography: David M. Walsh (DeLuxe Color). Assistant Directors: Fred T. Gallo, Terry M. Carr. Editor: Eric Albertson. Music: Mundell Lowe. Production Design: Dale Hennesy. Produced by Charles H. Joffe for United Artists. 87 minutes.

*Sleeper* (1973). Director: Woody Allen. Script: Woody Allen, Marshall Brickman. Photography: David M. Walsh (DeLuxe Color). Editor: Ralph Rosenblum. Production Designer: Dale Hennesy. Assistant Directors: Fred T. Gallo, Henry J. Lange, Jr. Special Effects: A. D. Flowers. Music by Woody Allen with the Preservation Hall Jazz Band and the New Orleans Funeral Ragtime Orchestra. Dr. Melik's house designed by Charles Deaton, architect. Produced by Jack Grossberg for Jack Rollins and Charles Joffe Productions. 88 minutes.

*Love and Death* (1975). Director: Woody Allen. Photography: Ghislain Cloquet (Deluxe Color). Script: Woody Allen. Editing: Ralph Rosenblum, Ron Kalish. Assistant Directors: Paul Feyder, Bernard Cohn. Special Effects: Kit West. Music: S. Prokofiev. Art Director: Willy Holt. Costume Designer: Gladys De Segonzac. Produced by Charles H. Joffe for Jack Rollins and Charles H. Joffe Productions. 85 minutes.

*The Front* (1976). Produced and Directed by Martin Ritt. Script: Walter Bernstein. Music: Dave Grusin. Photography: Michael Chapman (Panavision color). Art Director: Charles Bailey. Editor:

Sidney Levin. Assistant Directors: Peter Scoppa, Ralph Singleton. A Martin Ritt–Jack Rollins–Charles H. Joffe Production. Distributed by Columbia Pictures. 94 minutes.

*Woody Allen: An American Comedy* (1977). Produced and Directed by Harold Mantell, for Films for the Humanities, Inc. (P.O. Box 2053, Princeton, N.J. 08540). Narrated by Woody Allen. 30 minutes.

*Annie Hall* (1977). Director: Woody Allen. Script: Woody Allen and Marshall Brickman. Photography: Gordon Willis (Panavision DeLuxe). Editor: Ralph Rosenblum. Art Director: Mel Bourne. Animated Sequences: Chris Ishii. Assistant Directors: Fred T. Gallo, Fred Blankfein. Costume Designer: Ruth Morley. Produced by Charles H. Joffe for Jack Rollins and Charles H. Joffe Productions. Distributed by United Artists. 93 minutes.

*Interiors* (1978). Written and Directed by Woody Allen. Photography: Gordon Willis. Editor: Ralph Rosenblum. Production Designer: Mel Bourne. Assistant Director: Martin Berman. Costume Designer: Joel Schumacher. Produced by Charles H. Joffe for Jack Rollins–Charles H. Joffe Productions. Distributed by United Artists. 93 minutes.

*Manhattan* (1979). Director: Woody Allen. Script: Woody Allen and Marshall Brickman. Photography: Gordon Willis (black and white). Editor: Susan E. Morse. Production Designer: Mel Bourne. Costumes: Albert Wolsky. Music by George Gershwin, adapted and arranged by Tom Pierson; performed by the New York Philharmonic, conducted by Zubin Mehta, and the Buffalo Philharmonic, conducted by Michael Tilson Thomas. Assistant Directors: Frederic B. Blankfein, Joan Spiegel Feinstein. Executive Producer: Robert Greenhut. Produced by Charles H. Joffe for Rollins-Joffe Productions. Distributed by United Artists. 96 minutes.

*Stardust Memories* (1980). Written and Directed by Woody Allen. Photography: Gordon Willis. Editor: Susan E. Morse. Production Designer: Mel Bourne. Costumes: Santo Loquasto. Assistant Director: Frederic B. Blankfein. Executive Producers: Jack Rollins and Charles H. Joffe. Produced by Robert Greenhut for Rollins-Joffe Productions. Distributed by United Artists. 89 minutes.

*A Midsummer Night's Sex Comedy* (1982). Written and Directed by Woody Allen. Director of Photography: Gordon Willis. Editor: Susan E. Morse. Music by Felix Mendelssohn. Producer: Robert Greenhut. An Orion Pictures Company release through Warner Brothers. 85 minutes.

*Zelig* (1983). Directed and Written by Woody Allen. Director of Photography: Gordon Willis. Editor: Susan E. Morse. Music by Dick Hyman. Produced by Robert Greenhut. A Jack Rollins and Charles H. Joffe Production, released by Orion Pictures/Warner Bros. 84 minutes.

## DISCOGRAPHY

*Woody Allen: The Night-Club Years, 1964–68.* United Artists UA 9968, 1976.

# BIBLIOGRAPHY

Allen, Woody. *Don't Drink the Water*. New York: Random House, 1967.

———. *The Floating Light Bulb*. New York: Random House, 1982.

———. *Four Films of Woody Allen*. New York: Random House, 1982.

———. *Getting Even*. New York: Random House, 1971.

———. *Play It Again, Sam*. New York: Random House, 1969.

———. *Side Effects*. New York: Random House, 1980.

———. *Without Feathers*. New York: Random House, 1975.

Arnold, Gary. "Left-Over 'Memories,'" *Washington Post*, October 5, 1980.

Bettelheim, Bruno. *Freud and Man's Soul*. New York: Alfred A. Knopf, 1983.

Campbell, Joseph. *Myths, Dreams and Religion*. New York: E. P. Dutton, 1970.

Canby, Vincent. Review in *New York Times*, July 15, 1983.

Champlin, Charles. "Woody Allen Goes Back to the Well," *Los Angeles Times*, Calendar Section, February 15, 1981.

Corliss, Richard. "'A Little Faith in People,'" *Film Comment*, May–June 1979.

Denby, David. "Woody's Poison-Pen Letter," *New York*, October 13, 1980.

Dibbell, Carola. "Not Swept Away," *Village Voice*, June 4, 1979.

Gittelson, Natalie. "The Maturing of Woody Allen," *New York Times Magazine*, April 22, 1979.

Jacobs, Diane. . . . *But We Need the Eggs*. New York: St. Martin's Press, 1982.

Jung, Carl G. *The Archetypes and the Collective Unconscious*. 2nd ed. (Vol. 9, part 1 of *The Collected Works of C. G. Jung*.) Princeton: Princeton University Press, 1968.

Kael, Pauline. Review in *The New Yorker*, October 27, 1981.

Mantell, Harold. "The Words and Ways of Woody Allen," *Media & Methods*, December 1977.

Rich, Frank. "An Interview with Woody," *Time*, April 30, 1979.

Rogers, Carl. *Client-Centered Therapy*. Boston: Houghton Mifflin, 1951.

Sarris, Andrew. "Woody Doesn't Rhyme with Federico," *Village Voice*, October 1, 1980.

Schickel, Richard. "Woody Allen Comes of Age," *Time*, April 30, 1979.

Schwartz, Tony. "The Conflicting Life and Art of Woody Allen," *New York Times*, October 19, 1980.

Zinsser, William K. "Bright New Comic Clowns Toward Success," *Saturday Evening Post*, September 21, 1963.

# INDEX